WTF?
Why The fuss?

Special Thanks to My Mom, My Dad (Timothy D. Baker), Patricia Baker, Timothy J. Baker, Corleita Williams, John Branch, George Beeler, Sharmalee Burnett, Mikeal Chambers, Marcus Chavers, Andrea Cloud, John Edwards, Katie Van Lake, Melanie Fields, Jeff Granich, Nadjia Harris, Alma McCauley, Aisha McKinney, Ricardo Medina, Arthur Oates, Nilaja Parker, Tina Perkins, Stella Razo, Latonia Sanders and Sharae Smith for sharing you laughter, smiles, tears and sometimes agony over relationships and inspiring me to write this book.

EDITED BY:

Paul Gaszak

Disclaimer

Please understand that this advice is not expert advice or written in stone. I am in no way a relationship "expert". But, what I do have is a lot of experience and advice to share. Even the experts on relationship shows do not claim to know everything about love and relationships. Love can be daunting. Use the contents of this book only to gain more knowledge from someone who has either been there or is going through similar experiences.

0
Introduction

This book is the result of countless conversations with my girlfriends, male friends, lesbian friends, gay friends and everyone else in between. After years of going through great, good, okay, unhealthy and just plain old disastrous relationships, I have somehow become the ear that hears all of my friends' and associates' relationship issues. Perhaps because I have always been so real and open about my experiences in relationships, they feel comfortable opening up to me. What I have found is that when they ask me for my advice, I am surprised by how much I have learned when it comes to relationships. Every experience we have in our relationships teaches us something about that other person, and about ourselves. The theory is that we move on to each new romantic relationship with new knowledge. Unfortunately, not everyone can do this and we sometimes make the same mistakes, starting a never-ending, destructive cycle.

What's funny is that I often give out advice to my friends and laugh and shake my head at them when they don't even attempt to follow it and really mess things up. What's even funnier is that I don't always follow my own advice, but I have learned to think about the moves I make in a relationship and how they will affect the other person and, of course, myself. Writing this book is my way of sharing my advice with all women who need just one more voice to help them out in this thing we call love or, at least, what we hope is love. Everything that I am about to share with you is my own gospel. I also took some time out to conduct surveys and in-depth roundtable discussions with women and men to get some real answers to many pressing questions and issues.

This book is not a book about how to find a man and get married. I am not married so I have no right to tell another woman what she needs to do to get married and I can't stand when other unmarried people try to give marriage advice. This book is all about dating and having fun while doing so. Many women treat dating as the end all and be all of their lives and happiness which then makes it no longer fun. Dating is all about meeting someone new and having fun. If it leads to a great romance, then a relationship, then marriage, which is fabulous, if it doesn't, a woman should not feel like she has failed and life as she knows it is over.

Each chapter has a list of relevant songs from several genres. The songs may be remakes or covers, but I chose the versions that spoke to me the most. In my own life, no matter what I am going through, there is a song for it. These are not necessarily my favorite songs of all time, but they fit the topics in this book. They contain strong lyrics that you can most certainly take to heart. The lyrics speak to your heart in that moment that you are feeling a certain way.

I was also able to conduct an in-depth anonymous survey with a total of 100 men and women who revealed their likes and dislikes when it comes to dating. They also shared their major issues when it comes to dating. What I found most interesting about this survey is the information they shared about what made them fall in and out of love.

Think of this not as book but a conversation between friends. I really like to tell it like it is and I don't sugarcoat anything, so excuse me if the language is just a little bit harsh at times. But, there are some people that need to hear the truth in its raw form before they actually believe it. So, let's talk, ladies!

Part I

Let's Regroup

1
Maybe It's You

Write down five things that you like about yourself. **Go!**

_____

_____

_____

_____

_____

If you listed everything quickly, then you are off to a great start. If this took you five minutes or more to do, don't worry; this is why we have started here. If you couldn't think of one thing, put this book down and look for one that helps you to increase your self-esteem. I know that seems harsh, but you can't become one with someone else until you a whole yourself. No one is going to see the value in you if you don't see the value in yourself.

First, let's have a quick reality check as to why you always end up on the hurt end of a break up or, hell, you just can't keep a man. Yep, this is the part where I simply say, "Maybe it's you!" Some of you may have already begun to realize that your continuous demise in relationships mostly has to do with your own issues. I have certainly come to grips with mine and I am aware of what I should and should not do. But, there are some of you that are still delusional and think that it's all "his" fault. So, let me break down a few reasons why you keep falling victim to your own mistakes.

Your attitude stinks. This is the number one reason why a woman quickly turns off men. Most men can smell a bad attitude across the room and will avoid you like the plague. However, there are some of you who are able to mask your stank attitude for a while and then it rears its ugly head once you think you have him in your grips. I don't care how long you have been with a man, he will quickly get tired of the permanent scowl, your eyes rolling faster than a roller coaster, and your head and finger waving. In fact, you might find that your friends are just as miserable as you. Misery loves company, but it will surely drive a good man away.

You are just a pretty face. There is a saying that goes, "Show me a beautiful woman and I'll show you a man who is tired of screwing her." Of course, this is the edited version. Perhaps while you were concentrating on making sure your makeup, hair and wardrobe were perfect to attract the man of your dreams, you should have read a book or two. And by book, I don't mean the latest issue of Some Fashion Magazine (although I love those magazines too) or the latest romance novel. Now, I admit that I never leave the house looking like I just fell off of a turnip truck, but I also leave the house with intellectual confidence, meaning the ability to hold a conversation about almost any subject and, if I'm not fully versed on a topic, the ability to ask intelligent questions. The right man is not going to go for the pretty face too long and will be looking for much more from you if he wants to get serious.

You believe that the sun rises and sets on you. I remember sitting at a bar next to a couple that may have been about two or three dates into a possible relationship. The woman was constantly admiring herself in anything that would give off a reflection and focused the whole conversation on everything but the poor guy she was with. I could just read the disappointment on that man's face. I am willing to bet money that the relationship went absolutely nowhere beyond that bar or the bedroom.

You are not your biggest fan. Men can easily detect low self-esteem and lack of confidence in women. Most men will just keep it moving because they are not psychologists and do not have the ability to help you with your issues and also try to have a relationship with you. Even if he is a psychologist, I am sure that he wants to leave his work on the couch in his office. But there are some men that will use your lows to their advantage. This can be dangerous and further damage you mentally.

Now that I have pointed out some of the major reasons why you may be having problems in relationships and probably pissed you off, let's figure out how to turn things around for the better. Keep in mind that you know most of what I am discussing here; you just forget to apply it. What I hope will happen now is that you will be conscious of these issues and think before you subject the next man to any of them.

Problem: Your Attitude Stinks

Solution:

Let's first start with why your attitude stinks. We all have relationship baggage, but he first thing you need to realize is that the next man is not going to be like the last one unless you paint him that way. Many of my male friends have told me that the more a woman lets him know she holds him in low regards, the more he starts to fulfill her prophecy. Basically, if you are always assuming he is going to cheat on you, he will give you what you want and cheat. Men are just funny that way.

If you never have anything good or positive to say, you will quickly become the most unattractive woman that man has ever seen. No one wants to be around anyone who exudes negativity. Also, don't think your man is not paying attention when you are always throwing salt on everyone you know behind their backs. He will wonder if you are spewing the same negative venom about him as well.

The only way to come to grips with your anger and nasty disposition is to figure out how you became such a "Negative Nelly." Is there something you just don't like about you and don't want anyone else to discover? Are you harboring pain that was inflicted on you and unleashing it on anyone who gets too close to you so that they can't cause you any more pain? Are you purposely putting up walls for people to break down? This used to be my excuse for being hard on men. I would be as tough as nails until they bowed down to me; that is, the ones who actually put up with my crap. When I realized that I was ending up with men who were essentially my puppets, I grew tired of it. I really needed someone to stop me in my tracks, check me every now and then when I had gone too far, and simply tell me, "No, and I am tired of your bullshit." By the way, one man finally told me that and it made me stop and think about all of my silliness.

I know it will be hard for some of you, but you have to force yourself to be nice and pleasant until it feels natural. It can be as simple as smiling. Men love to see a woman smile because it lets them know they are doing something right and reassures them that you may actually like them. If you have yet to learn how to express your happiness in words, a smile goes a long way. I have overheard men say to women in crowded rooms that they couldn't take their eyes off of them because their smile was so beautiful. Men will look right past the chick that is sitting in the corner looking like she just stepped in dog shit with her new $800 pumps.

My advice is to find out why you are so unhappy and, in the meantime, try your best not to make innocent people fall victim to your anger. This could take a while and you may have to force yourself to be happy about even the smallest things, but it will be easier once you can detect those things that make you unhappy and rid your life of them. You may even want to seek professional help. Everyone needs a little therapy and you should not be embarrassed to seek it out. The bottom line is that you have to change your whole outlook on life to a positive one and open your mind to happiness. Remember, you have to be whole before you can become one with someone else.

Problem: You are just a pretty face
Solution:

Now, let's tackle the possibility that you may be a little shallow. Stop right now and ask yourself, "Would I date me and, if so, why?" If you can't answer that question then you have a serious problem. Men are looking for someone who brings more substance into their lives. Simply put, they are looking for someone that balances them out. The whole balancing thing comes into play when you discover for yourself what it is you have to offer a man. If all you can provide is sex and superficial conversation, you will always be someone's "fling."

When men are looking for a girlfriend who could possibly end up being a wife, they are looking for the total package just like women. They are looking for someone who is attractive in *their* eyes, nurturing, possesses a good amount of sensuality, career-minded or at least realistically ambitious, and is flexible when it comes to trying new things and adjusting to new situations. Men want women who can stand strong by their side and not just follow them. And every now and then they don't mind being led.

Now, there is a trick to figuring out if you balance your man out. The key is to figure out how you differ and how to bridge the gap without forcing your hand. First, think about some of his non-physical characteristics that stand out. For example, your man is very conservative. If you are very liberal and outgoing, then this could work. However, you can't force the man to jump on the bar and dance with you at a nightclub if that is just not his thing. In fact, you may have to tone your own rowdiness down to meet him halfway if he is willing to join you in your crazy world every now and then.

Another example could be that he only likes to attend sporting events and you like to attend art museums, the opera, and jazz concerts. If this man is really into you, he will take you to sporting events and educate you on the finer points of field goal percentages and you will do your best to enjoy it. The flipside is that you can show him that you are into him by treating him to the new impressionist art exhibit at the art museum.

The key is for you both to get involved in what makes your mate happy and enjoy it with them. It seems pretty easy to do but if everything is a struggle between you and your man when it comes to compromising on how you spend your time together, imagine how it will be when you have to decide where to live, what car to buy and how to raise kids. And this is the whole point when men are looking for their "Ms. Right." If you can't mesh with minor things, he will know right away that you can't mesh on major life experiences with him. One male friend of mine said being with his wife "is as easy as breathing." This pretty much sums it up.

Problem: You are not your biggest fan
Solution:

An astounding 70% of the women I surveyed have at some point depended on a man for happiness. This is quite frightening. If you are not happy with yourself, the last thing you need to do is go searching for that happiness in someone else. Men can quickly sense if a woman is down on herself and it is definitely a turn off. Low self-esteem and negative regard for yourself are things that *must* be fixed before you enter into any type of relationship with a man. At this point, you are just a shell of a woman that needs to be filled with all the goodness that life has to offer. What is dangerous is when that shell is filled with deceit, lies and abuse by a man who knows that he can do so and leave you even worse than before you started the relationship. You have to go into a relationship with your head on straight knowing who you are, how valuable you are and how you deserve to be treated.

Until you can truly love and appreciate yourself, no one else will. The best way to remedy this is by doing some true soul searching with either professional or spiritual help. If you can't afford therapy, go to your nearest bookstore or library and find books written by professionals that you can read and absorb at your own pace. You can also confide in a trusted friend who is willing to listen and support your efforts to becoming a better you. Although you will want to do most of your healing on your own, you should look to a strong support group or just one person to have your back while you transform.

It took me until I was about 32 to realize that I really didn't love myself at all. I thought that I did, but I was constantly doing self-destructive things. I didn't realize I had an issue until I finally had a bad break-up and felt an unfamiliar emptiness beyond that which a break-up will normally bring.

I was in a relationship with a man for three years. This man was wealthy, strong and exuded "power." We had become very close to the point where he shared all of his vulnerabilities with me. I met his entire family and he spent time with my family. In fact, our families had the chance to mix at his home. We eventually lived together. This is when everything seemed to change. He was no longer that nice, sensitive man that I loved. He became a mean tyrant who basically treated me like "the help". I was only there to serve his purposes and manage his home. He was cheating on me and really didn't even try to hide it because he figured I wasn't going anywhere. I began to lose touch with my own self-worth and felt like there was nothing I could do but accept this bad behavior. I became weak and he continued to break me down.

It wasn't until one day when he had just finished chastising me for buying the wrong thing at the grocery store that I realized that I was in no way a weak woman. He left after arguing with me and I ran to the bedroom crying. Suddenly, I lifted my head off of the bathroom sink and saw the tears. I also saw the pain in my own eyes for the first time. I got mad. Not mad at him, but mad at myself for allowing him to hurt me and change me. I decided it was time to go. I grabbed a tube of lipstick and wrote on the bathroom mirror, "The maid has left the building. Have a nice life!" I gathered whatever I could fit in suitcases and got out of that house and never went back. I was free, but the healing would take some time.

I had never been without a boyfriend and there was no one to immediately follow my ex and "rescue" me. I didn't know what to do with myself. I was miserable and did not know how to pull myself out of it. Luckily, I finally figured out that I was using what may or may not have been love from men to help me love myself. I was defining myself through my relationships. I sought out spiritual help and also forbid myself to get into another serious relationship until I got myself together.

If my own experience feels familiar to you, even if it is not that extreme, not only do you have my prayers, but I also hope that you will work to become whole in mind and spirit. There is nothing more attractive to a man than a woman who has a positive outlook about herself and on life. Remember, they are looking for the total package.

Chapter One Playlist

Kanye West – "Stronger"

Natasha Bedingfield – "Unwritten"

JazzyFatNastees – "Let It Go"

Amerie – "Gotta Work"

Kelly Price – "Tired"

Sade – "Soldier of Love"

Mary J. Blige – "No More Drama"

Des'ree – "You Gotta Be"

Chaka Kahn – "I'm Every Woman"

Jimmy Cliff – "I Can See Clearly Now"

India Arie– "I Choose"

Natasha Bedingfield – "Pocketful of Sunshine"

2
Have You Played Yourself Out?

Have you ever performed a search online for yourself? It may seem weird to some, but you should have no problem typing your own name aliases into a search engine to see what comes up. You need to not only search for textual info, but also any photos and videos. You never know where you may pop up. For those who really want to monitor their online presence, Google even allows you to set up alerts whenever your name pops up on the Internet.

What did you find? If you barely found anything but your old cheerleading photos from high school or an article you wrote for the local newspaper, then so far so good. However, if you found some raunchy stuff, then we have a problem. I'm going to stop beating around the bush and just tell you exactly how the internet can mess up your "game" and tell the wrong story about you before you even get to open your mouth.

Over the years, I have met women who were Playboy models, Urban Models (Smooth magazine, hip hop video vixens, etc.), exotic dancers, escorts and even porn stars. Now, I am not going to knock anybody's hustle, but there are some risks involved in these types of professions. Even if it has been years or even decades since you participated in certain activities or professions, if it was captured on photo or video, it is very likely that it will come back to haunt you. That stuff is etched in Internet history.

What's funny is that men always lust after and fantasize about being with women in these professions, but that's as far as it goes. They don't typically want to be "with" these women as in relationships or marriage. The reality is that men are taught, "You can't turn a whore into a housewife." I'm not saying you are a whore if you are engaged in any of these professions, but just realize that some men may view you as such.

The thing that will bother most men is that you have shown the world what he thinks only he should see. No man wants to be out with his woman on a romantic date only to have some random dude walk up and say, "Aren't you the girl from last month's edition of Big Booty and Boobies magazine?" Or even worse your man is over a friend's house and his screensaver on his computer is you bent over half naked.

Unfortunately, men have this insane idea that the woman that they will make their wife will be this angelic, virginal woman with a perfect past. At least this is how they need to feel in order to feel secure about being with you. In the back of their mind, they know that their girl has been with someone else before them but they block it out and act as if they are the first man she has ever laid eyes on. It is very hard for them to keep that thought tucked away when there are constant reminders that you may be a little "loose" even if you aren't.

The women that I know that have to deal with this reality have been on either end of the relationship spectrum. On one end, they will end up with a man who says he is cool with everything and then go ballistic the first time some guy recognizes them or when they see firsthand what it is that they do for a living. Those relationships either don't last long or they are off and on. On the other end of the spectrum, they end up with a man who is confident enough to know that it's just a means to an end (that is, if you haven't entangled the career into your everyday life) or it's something in the past. These men are far and few between and what's great is these are the men that will still commit to a relationship.

So, now I know some of you are either thinking back to what you have done in the past that a man may question or you are trying to figure out how to get those half naked photos off of the Internet. Don't panic! If there are things out there on the information super highway that you would like to erase, you may be able to do away with some of it. If they are photos that a friend took, simply ask them to take the photos down and hope that no one else has downloaded them. If the photos were for a print or online publication, good luck getting those out of circulation. Chances are, you signed a release and those photos now belong to that publication and they can do whatever they want with them. However, if the photos are old enough and no longer getting hits, you may be able to convince the publication to remove the photos.

The problem with being so exposed online is that your potential love interest can search you before your first date. The only remedy for this is to put it out there no earlier than the first date (if he doesn't bring it up) or by the second date. You don't want to seem like you are ashamed of anything (unless you are) or hiding anything. Just put it out there and see how he reacts. The best thing you could do is minimize that part of your life, talk about it quickly and then emphasize all of what you have going on for yourself that will make him forget about what he has seen.

If you are currently working in one of these industries and plan to keep working for a while, just know that you may have to deal with some men who just can't handle it and now you know why.

If you were thinking about auditioning at your local strip club or taking some saucy photos, let this be a cautionary tale. Your milkshake may bring all the boys to the yard, but that's the problem; your milkshake brings *all* the boys to the yard and your man won't feel special. Your chosen profession will always be the elephant in the room with you and your man.

Even if you are not in one of these professions and don't plan to be, there are some things you can do to take control of your online presence:

- Never take a photo with a drink in your hand even if you are out partying at a club. Be aware of who is snapping photos and where so that you aren't even caught in the background drinking. Photos like this can add up and turn into a long history of drinking making you appear to be a barfly who only has one goal in life: getting wasted.

- For goodness sakes, stop taking photos where you are purposely showing off your ass to the world even if you are fully clothed. I have seen social network profiles of women where every other picture is a "look back at it" photo. Just like I am shaking my head thinking, "Is that all there is to you?" so is that guy who may have been interested in getting to know you.

- Be careful what you post, "like" and comment on when you are on social networks. Certain comments will end up in search engines if they are clicked enough times. Think before you hit send.

- Try to limit how many social networks you belong to. Many of us still have MySpace pages and can't even remember the password in order to delete it. If you notice there are huge gaps between the times when you log on, perhaps you should just let that network go while you still remember the password. Don't forget, that those networks own your content so it is less likely to be spread all over the net or used for promotional purposes if your account is not active.

- Join networks that help to show off your business skills and expertise. Not only will it keep you relevant in the business world, but also your man will see that you give a damn about your career and future. Who wouldn't want a focused and career-minded woman?
- Try your best to limit your "friends" and "followers" to people you actually know. When you have a few thousand people following you, you have no idea who is truly trying to network and who could possibly use your info to sabotage you.
- Make it clear to your "friends" that you would rather not be tagged in photos or posts or set your accounts so that you have to approve both friendships and tags.

- Be careful what you review on some websites such as certain retail sites. Your review will pop up in search engines. If you have purchased something very personal, your business is all out for everyone to see
- Start your own website or blog about things that interest you and keep up with the content. It will more than likely be the first thing that pops up when someone searches you.
- Also, if you chose to go into one of the professions mentioned (if you haven't already started), use a name that is nowhere near your legal name. I honestly can't believe when people use their real name in adult and men's magazines and even in strip clubs. Not only are you exposing yourself to possible stalker issues, but you will never be able to separate that persona from who you really are. In fact, unless it's a professional career website, I recommend using nicknames on other social networks as well.

The whole point is to create as much positive content about you on reputable websites as possible so that all of the questionable stuff gets pushed further back in the search engine. Not too many people are going to go past the first two or three pages in search results unless they really want to dig up some stuff about you. Just be mindful of your online image or be ready to explain what everyone in the world can see. In other words, don't let the Internet "play" you out before you can show him who you really are.

Chapter Two Playlist

Destiny's Child - "Nasty Girl"

Fiona Apple - "Criminal"

2 Live Crew - "Hoochie Mama"

Jet - "Are You Gonna Be My Girl"

Kelis - "Milkshake"

Vanity - "Nasty Girl"

3
Get A Life

Picture this scenario: Girl is single and does nothing but go to school or work every day and not too much else. Girl meets Boy. Boy has interests, hobbies, and quite a well-rounded life beyond school and work. Girl becomes infatuated with Boy and maybe even falls in love. Girl somehow makes Boy's interests her own instead of having her own interests outside of the relationship. Girl makes Boy the center of her whole life with nothing else surrounding him. As time goes on, the relationship does not work out and Girl and Boy end up calling it quits. Boy carries on with all of the interesting things he had going on before and during his relationship with Girl and is just as happy as can be. Girl had nothing interesting going on before or during the relationship so she is miserable and depressed and not sure what to do with herself. Boy moves on to yet another great relationship while Girl is looking for someone to fill the void that Boy left.

We as women have a bad habit of rolling over and playing dead when we get into a relationship. We equate being in a relationship to giving up who we are. Somehow "I" vanishes for "We" and we no longer care about what made us happy individuals; that is, if we were happy individuals from the start.

Stop right now and write down five things that you enjoy doing by yourself or with girlfriends. **Go!**

_____

_____

_____

_____

_____

Now, I want you to commit to continue doing these things when and how you normally do them when you are in a relationship. You must have a life of your own before and during your relationships. You should have some amount of ambition not only because men love that about women, but because you will be more fulfilled as well. There has to be more to you beyond all of your responsibilities for your own sanity.

Now, I am not talking about going out and skydiving or alligator wrestling. I am talking about just having hobbies and taking part in activities that make you grow as a person and occupy your free time. There are obvious things that I like to do such as read, write and workout, but I am constantly looking for activities that are new to me and open my mind up to new cultures and experiences. For example, I love to go to museums- especially the kind where you get to touch things.

I am literally telling you to get a life because you better believe that your man is not going to totally give up his Wednesday nights with the boys, his Saturday afternoon flag football games and his video games after work for you. He may certainly cancel a few times to take you on a special date, but he is not giving up his hobbies all together. It is important for you to do the same. If you like to go out to dinner with your girlfriends after work on Fridays, then continue to do so and only break that tradition for your man occasionally. If you like to read quietly at home on Sunday afternoons, don't just drop it to talk on the phone with him for hours.

I think that one of the worst things we do as women is make ourselves overly accessible to our men and, believe me, some of them will pick up on this and take advantage of it. Most men will not always cancel their prior plans if their woman calls with something for them to do together unless it is really important and they know they will have hell to pay if they don't. However, women will totally blow off everything and everyone as soon as the phone rings and it's their man on the caller ID. This is extremely problematic. Once you start changing occasional plans, you slowly start to change your whole routine to accommodate his schedule. Again, unless a man is in a committed relationship with you and it is imperative that he does so, he is not changing up his life for you; you will have to get in where you fit in.

Also, your man does not need to know your every move. Some of you seem to have a GPS system up your ass and feel the need to report to your man every time you take a step. Now, stop and ask yourself if he does the same. Nope!

Your man does not report to you so STOP IT! This is not a game of cat and mouse. He should never have the right to manage your movements. This is a trust issue. If you have a man that needs to know your every move, look out because you could have a controlling asshole on your hands.

I had a boyfriend like that. He would have a fit if I didn't answer my phone or took too long to call back. Even worse, if I went somewhere without telling him. What a controlling dude, but at the time, I thought it was because he cared about me. If this is your line of thinking, you are sadly mistaken.

And, for goodness sake, stop answering the phone on the first ring and answering texts with lightning speed like you are back in high school. Doing either of these things makes a man think you have absolutely nothing else to do besides answer his calls. If you are busy, call or text him back later. It's okay to let a phone call go to voice mail every now and then. If you have your own life going on, chances are you are not sitting by the phone waiting on his calls anyway.

As far as interests go, it is not a good idea to pretend to be interested in something just because that is what the man in your life is into. I have dated men who were into things that I thought were interesting and I may have tried them just to make them happy and to say I did it, but I didn't make their interests my own because it just was not my thing. I can't stress enough how important it is that you stay true to yourself and don't let yourself become so consumed with the relationship that you lose who you are and are left lost if the relationship ends.

Chapter Three Playlist

Mary J. Blige - "Just Fine"

Nicki Minaj - "Moment For Life"

Nickelback - "If Today Was Your Last Day"

Bon Jovi - "It's My Life"

Kenny Loggins - "I'm Alright"

4
Holding It Down

For the purposes of this book, holding it down means that you are able to stand by your man, believe in him, and back him up. Believe it or not, men can easily equate their women with one basic accounting tool; the balance sheet. When a man is thinking about whether or not to stick around, at one point he will ask himself if you are an asset or a liability. Yep, it's that simple.

Before you start thinking that this is all about money; that is only about 10% of the equation. In order to keep a man's interest, you need to prove your value. For example, if you never support any of his passions, you may be a liability. I'm not talking about that time when he wanted to buy a scale model of the Titanic and have a re-dedication ceremony in the pool. I'm talking about when he wants to change his career or even his way of life for himself and for the benefit of the relationship and you barely hear him out.

Men take score each time you turn your nose up at their dreams, hopes and wishes and eventually they realize that you will never have their back. Of course they are going to come up with ideas and plans that you don't agree with, but this is where you prove how strong of a woman you really are. Hear him out and if it's something that you just don't agree with or feel is destined to fail, share your thoughts with him. Perhaps you can compromise or maybe you'll get your way and change his mind all together. You don't want to be the one to just kill your man's ambition. If you never have any encouraging words for your man, he will soon start to realize this. His next move may be on to another woman who will hold him down.

Now, let's talk finances. Most men will consider a woman's stage in life such as her career, mental capacity, and even her earning potential. About half of the men that I surveyed preferred a woman who can contribute to the household finances. It creates more opportunities for you both to reach goals together and live a less stressful life. It's great to have a man that provides, but it is also great to be able to add to the financial wellbeing of the relationship.

The biggest cause of most of the drama in relationships is disagreements over money. Either someone is spending too much of it, someone is not making any of it or someone wants to control all of it. Money issues can be the root of many problems in a relationship.

I have dated my share of wealthy men and you better believe that I loved getting gifts and knots of cash to go buy whatever I wanted to buy. I even considered quitting my job for a guy that gave me that good old line, "As long as you are with me, you don't have to work." When he came to me with that line, of course I was thinking about how my life would be less stressful if I didn't have to worry about paying my bills. If my man was going to pay all of my expenses and also provide me with all the luxuries that I liked, that seemed like an offer that I couldn't refuse. All I was thinking about was the present and not the future. What if the relationship didn't work out? Once the man is gone, so is his money. I'm glad I put the kibosh on that nonsense. Eventually, I would have grown tired of asking for money for things that I needed and wanted.

Ladies, there is nothing like having your own money. I'm not saying that you should just shun any man that wants to give you a hand every now and then or even spoil you. It's nice to get gifts but allowing someone to totally support you financially takes away any power you may have in the relationship. There are exceptions to this rule. This rule changes up a little once you are married, but if you don't want to compromise the financial well-being that you have built up for yourself, you shouldn't have to. Men appreciate a woman that can hold it down financially; this is considered an asset.

Men don't mind spoiling us when they are able and help you out when things get a little tight, but what they don't want is a "Gimme Girl" who always has her hand out to every man with which she is involved. This is where that whole financial liability issue comes in. Even if you are with a wealthy man, he will certainly take note that you always have your hand out. There is one rule that I always follow: if you can't buy that item for yourself then don't expect him to. If you can't go and buy your own Gucci bag, why do you expect him to buy it? You aren't even about that life, but you want a man to give it to you. What you are doing is begging. The only time you get a pass is on birthdays and holidays. Let the man decide if he wants to shower you with gifts.

In fact, the less you ask for, the more you get. I once had a man that I never asked for anything. I am the queen of marking catalog items that I am considering purchasing by folding the pages. He watched me do this one night and somehow got his hands on the book after I finally put it down. He ordered everything that I had picked (although some things had to be exchanged) and surprised me with the package. I was a little taken aback but it gave him so much joy to finally be able to do something for me. He said that he could not figure out for the longest time what he could do to surprise me until he saw me with the catalog. Now, don't you all go home and start marking your Neiman Marcus catalogs for your man to see. This is something that I had (and still do) a habit of doing and absent-mindedly did in front of my man. What's important is that he knew that I was marking things so that *I* could buy them and I wasn't *expecting* him to buy them.

If your man is truly in tune to who you are and what makes you happy, he will do things for you without you asking. It may not be exactly what you want, but you better appreciate it all the same because this is no easy task for a man. But, as soon as you start constantly putting your hand out, the less he may want to do for you.

Chapter Four Playlist

Rick Ross ft. Chrisette Michele & Drake – "Aston Martin Music"
Ne-Yo – "Champagne Life"
Destiny's Child – "Independent Women"
Jennifer Lopez – "Love Don't Cost a Thing"

5
That Damn List

You need to figure out what you are looking for in a man. This is the part where you take out that wish list of qualities that you started writing when you were nine years old. If you still have things like "he brings me my glass slipper when I lose it" on the list, boy do we have work to do. Tear up that list that you have either written down or etched in your brain and let's start all over again.

One thing we need to distinguish is our wants from our needs. We do this all the time when we are making other decisions like buying clothes, groceries, and cars. So, why wouldn't we use the same line of thinking when we are choosing the person that we want in our lives? It's like all rationale goes out the door when we are attempting to choose the right man.

Write down five qualities that you are looking for in a man. **Go!**

_____

_____

_____

_____

_____

Now, and this is a biggie, look at that list and see if you can meet any of your expectations that you require of a man.

As women, we have a really bad habit of holding men to higher standards than we hold ourselves. For instance, requiring that a man be gainfully employed, have the body of a pro athlete and possess a high level of cultural awareness when you are broke, out of shape and clueless beyond reality shows is a bit of a stretch. You can't possibly expect perfection from a man when you are nowhere near it. So, now let's rethink this whole list thing.

I have learned that when you want something bad enough, you write it down and you continue to speak it into existence. So, grab a piece of paper and let's get started. You will be making two lists. The first one will be a list of what you have to offer a man. This could be anything from emotional support to great sex (please, don't let this be the only thing on the list), but be honest with yourself. After you are done making a list of what you have to offer, now think about what you need from a man that compliments what you have to offer. For example, if you can offer emotional support then you may be looking for a man who is ambitious and will appreciate that support. Or if you are adventurous, you may want to look for a man who possesses that same quality. In other words, make your list of requirements compliment who you are as a person and what makes you happy.

The whole point of this is to be realistic. Women constantly complain about men not meeting their standards, but we forget that we need to meet standards too. Men have lists as well and if you don't measure up, you won't make the team. Hell, you won't even get to tryout with a man who has his shit together.

Knowing what you need from someone going into the relationship will save you a lot of heartache and pain later. If you know that the person you are dating is a homebody and you like to go out and do things together, you either try to find a happy medium or keep it moving if he is just not into it. This also works in the reverse. For example, if you meet a man that wants a woman that is already established in her career and financially stable and you are not there yet, let him know up front and you both can decide if things will work out. Knowing who you are, what you want and having realistic expectations from your man makes for a great relationship.

    Let's not forget that your list is not written in stone. There will be a time when you will have to re-evaluate what you are looking for in a man or your "type." This happens for many reasons, one such reason being maturity. As you grow mentally, you will be able to see past the obvious and really see qualities in people that you would have never noticed before. You will realize that what you are looking for may not come in the package that you were expecting. You will also find that your list will become shorter or even change as you experience different types of men and relationships.

    No one can tell you what to put on your list. Your wants and needs should balance out and you must remain flexible. Sometimes what we think we need is really something that we want. It's up to you to figure out which is which.

Chapter Five Playlist

Shine Down - "Simple Man"

TLC - "No Scrub"

ZZ Top - "Sharp Dressed Man"

Destiny's Child - "Soldier"

Womack & Womack - "Baby I'm Scared of You"

Weather Girls - "It's Raining Men"

Mary J. Blige - "Real Love"

Diana King - "Shy Guy"

6
Reevaluate Your Circle

As much as we hate to admit it, our friends have a great influence on our love relationships. A friend will express how much of a loser your man is or they will give you enough hints to let you know they are not feeling him. So, how do you distinguish between someone who is being a "hater" and someone who is concerned about you? This is a very delicate situation. It's no secret that there are some women who hate to see another woman happy and some of these women might very well be parading around as your "friends."

There is one test to see if you have a frienemy (an enemy posing as a friend) among your ranks. For the first part of the test, you will bring a guy around your friends, especially the questionable ones. This guy will be a guy that you know is a certified douche bag or asshole. You know he will show his ass and be the jerk that you know him to be so sit back and watch but make sure you look as miserable as possible. The next day, see who has something negative to say. You may have a friend that is brave enough to pull you aside during the gathering and tell you how shitty the guy is behaving. I know many of my friends who may even tell him to his face. If no one has anything negative to say, don't just assume that they are all praying for your demise. There is more.

The second part of the test is to bring a really great guy around these same friends and see how they react. There may be one person out of the group that may reveal themselves. They will do this by challenging half of the things this man says, rolling their eyes when he speaks, and being just plain disrespectful to him. They may even go so far as telling you how lame he is or even that he is not right for you. This will be that Oprah Winfrey "ah ha" moment. This person may not be all for your happiness. They want you to stay unhappily single with them. This goes for male friends too, except your straight male friends may have their own motives for wanting to keep good men out of your life such as wanting you for themselves.

These tests help to determine who is for you and who is against you as far as relationships only. This is not me giving you the go ahead to shut down everyone who turns their nose up at the men in your life. The whole point is to manage your friends around or out of your relationships. At the end of the day, the only people that need to be all up in your relationship mix is the two people involved.

You have to know how to express the boundaries to your friends. One thing I have always done is listen to the positive as well as the negative things my friends say and let them know that I have heard them and consider their thoughts. This is when my gut would kick in and I had to really think about the place where those thoughts were coming from. Most times my gut was right, but other times it was dead wrong. Most times, I had to step outside of the relationship and look at it from all angles. If I didn't like what I saw then perhaps my friends were on to something and I needed to sit up and pay attention. If I saw nothing wrong, then I kept it moving and made it clear to my friends that my relationship was still going strong.

Once again, you have to set boundaries and make it very clear what you will not tolerate from your friends. If they can't validate their claims about your relationship or anything that has to do with your personal life, then they need to keep their mouths shut. However, if they have good reason to believe that you may be losing in your relationship and can back it up with genuine love and concern then listen to their words and then listen to your gut.

Whatever you do, don't become that sometimes friend who quickly disappears from the face of the earth when you have a man. It also means that you need to go back and read Chapter 2 about getting a life. If you have a pattern of disappearing from your friends and family when all is good in your love life and then reappearing when the relationship ends, folks will start to notice. You may be able to get away with it a couple of times but, eventually, the people you need in your life for moral support will get tired of your yo-yo ways. It is very important to strike a healthy balance between coupledom and individuality. Ditching everyone when you get a man in your life only to come back with your tail tucked between your legs when the relationship is over is not a good look.

At the end of the day, your friends were there before Mr. Right came along and they will be there if he should go. That is, if you respect them and they respect your relationship. Keep this in mind and you will have one less thing to stress about in your relationship.

Chapter Six Playlist

Destiny's Child – "Girl"

Rihanna – "Umbrella"

Janet Jackson – "Alright"

Brandy – "Best Friend"

7
Be A Head-Turner

Here is where we separate the women from the girls. You can't expect to catch a great guy if you do not brand yourself correctly. I am a firm believer that you get back what you put out in the world. This theory also holds true for what type of men will come into your life and how they will approach you.

In Chapter One you evaluated who you are and what makes you happy. Once you find happiness and know what it is that you want and need out of life, you will have a natural glow and attract like-minded people, including men. In fact, you will find that you will smile more and just have an overall pleasant disposition. I know that we can't all be "Suzy Sunshine" every day, but the majority of your days will not be filled with doom and gloom and you won't be projecting all of that badness into the world. But, here is where this can all fall apart for you.

Even if you have found inner peace and happiness, you can truly screw this up by letting the outside overshadow the inside. Men are visual creatures. You have to capture their eyes before you capture their hearts and minds. So this is where all of the female kryptonite that you have in your arsenal comes out. The key to attracting the man that you really want is to appear to be the woman he really wants. I don't mean you are faking anything, but you have to remember that this man is going to be choosing you before you even open your mouth and show him how awesome you really are.

The first thing is to wear pretty panties, but you won't be wearing them to give up to the guy. You are wearing them to jumpstart your sexiness. Picking out the prettiest panties in the drawer and wearing them under a business suit, work uniform or even sweat pants will automatically add a little something extra in the way you walk that no one will know about but you. So, ditch those ugly granny panties and take a trip to the lingerie store and get sexy with your under things. During your next trip to the lingerie store, you should only be looking for lace and the least amount of it as possible.

Now let's discuss what you are going to wear over those panties. Always keep in mind that you are a walking advertisement for yourself. If you personify sleaziness, you will attract less desirable men. You must know the difference between sexy and slutty. Think about how men talk to you when you are out in a social gathering. If you are at an upscale event and the women who are dressed more conservatively are getting all of the male attention, you may be dressed inappropriately. If you go the club and men tend to want to reach out and touch you more than the other women you are with, or if they are saying tasteless things that blatantly reveal that they want to have sex with you, you may dressed just a little slutty.

Now, don't go tearing up all of your miniskirts just yet, there is a way to fix all of this. You better believe that I had my confused period when I dressed in what I thought was sexy and could not understand why men were being so disrespectful to me. Let's go from head to toe.

Hair & Makeup

When it comes to hair and makeup, men tend to see some looks as an indication of a high-maintenance chick. Wearing multiple shades of eye shadow that are not blended well and tons of lip gloss (men hate that sticky feeling on their face and lips) may turn some men off. Hairstyles that look like you have five different hairstyles going on or hair that doesn't move (unless you wear your hair really short) are also turn offs. Men simply want to see an enhancement of your natural self not some totally different person that you created. Basically, if you look like a totally different person when you take off your makeup and your hair is not done, you can really disappoint some poor unsuspecting guy. If the relationship gets underway and you finally spend the night together, he will be in for a rude awakening if the woman he went to sleep with is not the same woman he wakes up with. In fact, if you went to bed with all the fakeness on, most of it will be on the pillow anyway.

The best thing you can do if you are clueless about makeup application is to go to your local makeup counter and get help.[1] Be careful because many times the makeup artists at those counters will try to really make you over. Let the artist know that you just want to learn how to apply your makeup so that it doesn't take you an hour to do so and you don't look "made up."

---

[1] I am a big fan of the MAC makeup artists. They explain how to apply the makeup and the products are high quality and easily adjusted for intensity.

When it comes to hair, find a style that is easy on the eye and easy to maintain. If you have long hair, stop wearing it in ponytails, get it cut into layers and let it flow. Guys love that whole lingerie model tussled hair look. They are looking at that hair and imagining their hands running through it. If you have short hair, stick with a soft style that doesn't look like it will poke someone's eyes out. This means, save the spikes for the next rock or rap concert that you attend. Your hair should not be the center of attention or a conversation piece.

For ladies who like to wear hair extensions-like yours truly-this is always a dilemma. For the most part, men understand that we sometimes have a little something extra going on up there. The key is to not go overboard. Don't put so much extra hair on your head that you need a neck brace. Also be careful about the length[2]. There are lots of rules to follow that go along with your body type. There are countless websites[3] and magazine articles that will give you all the tips you need.

---

[2] The best thing to do is consult with someone who is an extension expert and who will be realistic about the appropriate length for you.

[3] *Allure* magazine's website, allure.com offers great tips on choosing hairstyles and length based on your face shape.

Hair color is important as well. Stay away from the exotic colors like purple, fire engine red and green unless you are doing a hair runway show the next day. You want the extensions to match your natural hair color as closely as possible. If it means color treating the artificial hair or your hair, you will have to do so or leave the whole thing alone. Men notice these things and will even discuss it with the other men around them. So, not only will the women be talking shit about you, the men will get a chuckle about you being "unbeweavable."

Your Body

Before we move onto your clothing, let's make sure everything looks as good as possible under those clothes. When was the last time you went to the gym? I know some of you will balk at that question because you think I am telling you to lose weight. Not even. What I am suggesting is that you look as healthy as you can and you feel comfortable in your skin. If everyone on this planet had the same body type, it would be a pretty boring place. If you look toned and healthy at whatever size you are, there is a man checking you out. In fact, men love to see curves on a woman. It's an animal instinct to be attracted to mates who appear to be healthy and can help to produce healthy strong children. You need to tone what you have and get to a healthy body image that you can feel great about. This advice is not just for my curvy ladies, but the skinny ones too. There was a time when I fell below 100 pounds due to stress and folks thought I was about to drop dead any minute. Men don't want a woman who looks like she needs to eat. Get some protein in your body and tone it up as you add it. You don't just want to be healthy for outward appearances; you want to be healthy so that maybe you can stop subtracting years from your life.

Your Clothing

How do you dress to impress? If you want to attract a quality man, you need to look like a quality woman. This does not mean that you have to go out and burn up your credit cards buying expensive clothes. A lot of what you need is probably in your closet already and you just need to modify it.

First, think about what is age appropriate. There comes a point when the clothes that you are used to wearing just don't work anymore. If you are over 30 and still wearing dresses that come just to the top of your nipples and just to the bottom of your ass, you may be setting yourself up for failure. There is nothing wrong with showing a little skin, but when you can't sit or bend over without everyone knowing exactly what's going on under your clothes, you are putting the wrong message out there. To keep it real, this type of clothing at any age is not sending the right message.

Dressing inappropriately can also mean that your timing is off. How many times have you been at a gathering and someone clearly did not get the memo about the proper attire for the event? If you can't think of a time, it may have been you. If you have ever gone to a funeral or religious ceremony with a tight mini dress on, your timing was off. If you have ever attended a professional networking event with distressed jeans and a tank top, your timing was off. To avoid situations like this, every woman should own at least two suits, one black suit and one in a neutral color. A nice wrap dress in a solid neutral color is also a great piece to have in your closet. You should own at least two pairs of trousers, one black pair and another pair in a neutral color. You should own a few blouses with sleeves and short sleeves that are not transparent or full of glitter or anything else that is distracting. You should own a couple pairs of jeans that do not have holes in them or have a bunch of embellishments that are not so tight that people can tell even when you have a thong on under them. Anything else that you have in your closet is a plus if it compliments your body and how you feel about yourself. You should also own a few pairs of shoes in black, browns and other neutral colors that have no more than a four-inch heel.

Now, let's talk about heels for a bit. As a former tomboy, I didn't truly begin to grasp the power of heels until I started dating in my 20s. There is something about wearing heels that exudes sexuality in a woman. They help your posture by forcing you to stand up straight with your shoulders back and holding yourself up with good posture makes you appear more confident. However, walking in heels gracefully takes practice. There are women who can walk in heels and then there are women who can *catwalk* in heels. Knowing how to do the latter is a plus. One way to not look like an absolute fool when you are wearing heels is to wear your new shoes around the house for a few hours before you wear them out or just get into the habit of wearing heels more. If you can't get your rhythm together, put them back in the box and take them back to the store. You also need to know how high you can go. Personally, I can wear up to a six-inch platform heel and walk like I am in sneakers. Not every woman can do this. You have to try out different heel heights to know what works. You don't want to be in pain all night, but you still want to look sexy. My only hard and fast rule is to leave the flats and kitten heels (one and a half inches) at home if you want men to do a double take when you walk into the room. Of course, if there is a medical reason why you can't wear heels, then you better have a killer walk that you can pull off in whatever type of shoe you wear. And please don't forget to keep your feet looking fabulous all year round and not just in the summer.

If you are still clueless about putting your clothing ensembles together, seek some help. This help can come in the form of one of your more stylish girlfriends, a male friend, a professional wardrobe stylist or even the sales associates at your favorite retail clothing stores. I will be the first to admit that I am fashion illiterate and will seek help in any form. Just make sure that you are comfortable in your skin and your clothes, but also be open to try a new look that you may not normally wear.

Your Behavior

A woman can be picture of perfection, but can totally turn off everyone in the room with her overall behavior. I know I am no angel when it comes to the words that come out of my mouth. I can swear and cuss with the best of them. However, a "lady" needs to know when to turn the switch on and off. Appearing to be loud and boisterous in a social gathering that consists of a mixture of people is not a good look. If you know that alcohol brings out this type of behavior in you then you need to keep the drinking to a minimum or leave it alone altogether. Being the loudest person in the room is not the way to get attention you should be getting. Also, you may want to mind how you treat the people that serve you. I remember being on a dinner date with a man who was so rude to the waiter that I was instantly turned off and wanted to end the date. I can even recall being out with my girlfriends and one of the women just couldn't be satisfied with any of the food that *she* ordered and complained and returned not one but two plates. I had to wonder if the reason why she was always without a mate was because of how she behaves on dates if this was any indication of that behavior. Remember that the man of your dreams could be just across the room watching you and you're turning him completely off by being less than a lady. If you are not sure what is and isn't appropriate behavior in public, there are plenty of websites[4] and books[5] that give advice on etiquette in any situation. Even in situations where you are not actively looking for a mate or know that you may attract men, you should always carry yourself in a way that is classy and respectful.

Remember that looks are not the *total package.* Some men have told me that the way a woman looks and how she carries herself in all situations (her poise) is a good gauge of whether or not she is "wife material." I may seem crazy but, some of them have even claimed to see a glowing light around that special woman the first time they saw her. You may not actually become their wife, but you will be the type of woman that they actually want to spend time with and get to know. Getting the man's attention is only half of the battle. If a man does not see what he is looking for in you, it will be hard to change his mind so first impressions are very important.

---

[4] EmilyPost.com
[5] Emily Post's *Etiquette:Manners for a new world* 18th Edition is a great investment

Men are sizing us up just like we are sizing them up. The key is to stand out without looking like you are starving for attention.

Chapter Seven Playlist

James Blunt – "You're Beautiful"

Teairra Mari – "Body"

Joss Stone – "Head Turner"

Shania Twain – "Man I feel Like A Woman"

Destiny's Child – "Bootylicious"

Strings ft. Keith Sweat – "All Eyes On Me"

Leah LaBelle – "Sexify"

Part II

Happy Dating

8
Mr. Wrong

I couldn't possibly live with myself if I sent you out in the world without knowing which men to avoid. I have compiled my own list of men to avoid and descriptions so that you can quickly recognize them. Please note that this is not an exhaustive list, but these are the type of men you can spot right away and avoid a lot of heartache and pain.

Mr. Gigolo

If you like to pamper your men and buy them nice things, this guy will totally capitalize on it and leave you in the dust as soon as you tighten your wallet. Chances are he has several other women doing the same things for him that you are. He starts out like any normal guy paying for dates, but soon finds excuses for you to pay. Then, before you know it, you are financing him, his friends and maybe even the next woman who is assuming his is spending *his* money on her. As soon as you notice that this dude is constantly in your pockets, repossess all of your shit and send him on his way.

The Stalker

This man will ask you for your number and then call you about seven times before you even get home. He will immediately follow your every move on every social network and make it known to everyone that he is digging you before you even go out on a date. He will call and text you all day even when you have made it clear that you are busy. He may even insist on coming to your place just to get even further into your business. Basically, this dude is a-noy-ying. We all love attention but this kind of attention is damn near grounds for a restraining order. The only way to get rid of this guy is clearly tell him you are not interested and you wish to have no further contact with him. Just make sure you give your family and close friends a good description of him just in case he decides to get a little crazy. I am totally not kidding about this.

Mr. Storyteller

This guy will lie about everything, even when he doesn't have to: his nationality, his education, the names of his pets, etc. He is trying very hard to be more interesting than he really is and will say anything to wow you. In fact, he has been telling lies so long that he has convinced himself that they are true. If he will lie about simple things that really don't matter, what else will he lie about? He will also lie to you about other people so check your facts before you start judging people the way he wants you to judge them. No one likes a liar and you should just cut him loose before he tells a lie that could get you in trouble.

Mr. Smooth

Hi is the sexiest man in the room and he knows it! He knows exactly how to carry himself and what to say to women to make them fall at his feet. Don't join those other women down there licking his wing tips. In fact, it will bother him that you are the only woman paying him no mind and you can quickly flip the script on him. Men like this are used to getting lots of attention from women and will not care if you are not giving him attention at a given point in the relationship and go out and get it elsewhere. He enjoys being chased by women and loves having his pick of the litter. Now, I am not saying pick the most undesirable man in the room just because you don't want to get your feelings hurt, but don't play into the ego of a man like this.

Mr. Convict

Working in the legal field, I am always puzzled by the women who continue to attend court dates and save themselves for a man who is in jail or constantly in and out of jail. With so many men in the world that do not have criminal records, why would you run after a man who may never be gainfully employed or respected in? There is no way in hell that you should be spending your hard earned money and running to court dates and jail visits for a man that will not do the same for you. Now, I know there are simple things that anyone could get locked up for but a man that is constantly in and out of jail for nonsense is drama that you just don't need. Not to mention he could possibly get you caught up in his legal mess. So, if you meet a guy like this, kindly excuse yourself. If your man is locked up now, kindly tell him not to drop the soap and not to call you collect anymore. If there are kids involved, it's a different ballgame and you need to decide how much contact a man with a questionable character should have with your kids.

Mr. Drunken Druggie

This man can come in all walks of life: rich, middle-class, poor, old, young, and any race. Be on the lookout for a man that feels the need to take a drink every day. I can understand the occasional beer or shot to unwind after a hard day at work, but *every* day can't be hard. If alcohol is his solution to every problem or he can't have a good time without being drunk, this is a problem. A man that does drugs may not expose himself right away. He may want to feel you out and then spring it on you later. You should not be made to feel like a lame if you don't drink more than socially or take a toke of marijuana or a bump of cocaine. If he does drugs and you are against them, then this is not the man for you. There is no need to judge him, read him bible scriptures or slip "Just Say No" pamphlets into his brief case. He needs to get help and, until he is clean, you should go your separate ways.

Mr. Sky Cap

Men like to make it seem like women are the only ones who have baggage. Let me tell you, there are men out there carrying a whole matching set of baggage down to the train case. These men will do the same things that women do such as constantly talk about their exes and what they did wrong. They will also kill your ears with all that nonsense about how women don't know what they want and how much they have tried to be a good man. True, many of us don't know what we want, but who wants to hear that bull all night. These types of men have some deep rooted issues with women that they need to reconcile and until they do, let them simmer and perhaps one day they can prove that they are a good man for you without all the whining.

Mr. Down-low

This man has come to light in the last decade or so. "Down low" means this man is really a gay man pretending to be straight. He may have many reasons for doing this, but the obvious reason is that he is not ready to come out of the closet yet. He is using you as a prop to continue to fool his friends and family who may already have some hint of his homosexuality. The men that are good at hiding their true sexuality are probably some of the most masculine men you'll ever meet. But, believe me, he will do something that will clue you in to what is really going on. I have watched some of the most masculine business men in suits *admire* another attractive man from across the room in a way that suggests that he is not just giving him props for the nice shoes he has on. This is when it helps to get to know his friends and see how they interact together. Also, a man with a lot of female friends may not be a Mr. Smooth; he may be more comfortable with the fairer sex. At any rate, if you find out your man is homosexual, bow out gracefully (no need to put his business out in the streets) and make him your new shopping mate.

Mr. Sticky Fingers

I remember dating a guy who would take things from me that he didn't think I would miss. I have a nice size CD collection (yep, I still have those and will keep them), but I know when there was a disc missing. Every time this dude would leave my house, a few days later, I noticed a CD or two would be missing. So, I set a trap and it turns out he was not only stealing my CDs but also items from my medicine cabinet like pills. He was dumb enough to let the medicine cabinet kleptomaniac confession slip out when I confronted him. When you are dating someone new, keep a close eye on your belongings. In fact, if you don't trust someone, they should not be in your house until you do. A thief is a thief and if you let him any deeper into your life, there is no telling what else he will take from you.

Mr. Prison Guard

This guy will disguise his insecurity with "caring" about you. He will want to know where you are all the time. He will also have a stone cold fit if you don't answer your phone or call him back within a certain time. You will think that it is cute at first, but when you find yourself sweating like a hooker in church when you see a missed call from him an hour earlier, you have a problem. This man does not care about you; he is insecure and can't handle you having your own life outside of your relationship with him. Many times he has become this type of man after a woman has cheated on him and all women after her are not to be trusted out of his sight. This will be one of the most stressful relationships ever if you let it go on. You will need to cut him off cold turkey and let him know why so maybe the next woman doesn't have to suffer *as much*.

Mr. Workaholic

We all enjoy a man who works hard for his money and is career-driven. That should be on all of our lists of desires. However, there are some men who eat, sleep, and breathe their work. There is nothing that will ever come between them and their work; not even you. All work and no play makes for a boring and one-sided relationship. Sure we all have times when work takes over our lives, but if your man is involved in his work more than 75% of the time and there seems to be no end in sight, it may never change. If a man is really into you, he will make time for you even if he just picks up the phone and chats with you between meetings. After days of him not returning your phone calls or texts because he is working overtime and you just want to go out for coffee, send him an email explaining while you will be having coffee with someone else.

Mr. Man-Child

You can also call him the "Mama's Boy." This boy has never grown up and expects you to take over where his mother left off in raising him. Some of them are still being raised by their mothers and you will never be able to break through that dilemma so don't even try. Whether you have kids of your own or not, who wants to raise a grown man too? Most of the time, these are the men who still have no idea what they want to do with their lives, always live in the moment and lack any type of adult skills such as cleaning up after themselves. The only thing you can do is throw him back in the pond like a baby fish because he is not ready for an adult relationship.

Mr. Pro-Creator

This guy loves to literally spread his love around. I remember dating a guy who had one kid when we met, but by the time the relationship had pretty much imploded he had about four or five kids. He knew better than to tell me about all those kids in the beginning because he knew I would totally jump ship. I am not against a man with kids, but the Pro-Creator usually has kids by multiple women. So, not only do you have to get along with the kids, you may or may not get along with all of the mothers. Oh, and, be careful with men with kids who are still infants. The relationship may not be completely over on one or both sides. For women with or without kids, why would you want to put yourself through all of the drama of all of those people in the middle of your relationship if you really don't have to? God forbid you get pregnant by this guy too. You will just be on his list of women he has to pay child support; that is, *if* he can pay all of you. Some men will just come out and tell you about their situation, but there are some who will hide it until you are all in love and then you find out.

You have to question the morality of any man who would deny his children. It's really despicable. If you want to stick around and play stepmom about three, four, five, or more times over, more power to you. For those who don't want the drama, there are still men out there with no kids, kids by the same woman or who don't deny that they even have children.

Mr. Married Man

How would you like it if some hussy were sniffing around your husband? This is the ultimate karma killer. Don't think for one minute that it is okay to involve yourself with a married man no matter what he tells you. They will say anything to play down the sanctity of their own marriage. You'll get hit with, "We both do our own thing", "We are in the process of separating", "My wife doesn't care what I do", "I'm leaving her" and "I am hoping you can be the next Mrs. ____." Don't believe any of that shit. Until that man signs on the dotted line or is legally separated, he is off limits. The worst thing you can do is intrude on a woman who may be working hard to make her marriage work. Even if the wife is clueless, causing another woman the devastation that you will eventually cause is just the ultimate sin. He will never leave his wife for you and if he does you run the risk of having one of the worst relationships ever because you will never trust him and vice versa. As soon as you know that a man is married, that is your cue to exit stage left and find a man who isn't hiding his wedding ring in his pocket.

The Abuser

You'll notice that this man is not a "Mr." This man does not even remotely deserve that kind of respect. There are five common types of abuse in relationships. The most common type is physical abuse. It is never okay for a man to hit you or have any type of physical contact that causes you pain. Emotional abuse occurs when you already have a low self-esteem or if the man has a need to cut down a woman that he feels is too strong. The abuser will continue to make you feel low by criticizing and belittling you. Financial abuse can occur one of two ways: 1) the abuser controls all of the money and makes you ask for money or you have to explain how you are spending the money or 2) you are the only one contributing financially while the abuser does absolutely nothing to contribute to the relationship whether it's monetary or physical chores. Educational abuse is when your mate does everything in their power to keep you from furthering your education or doing anything that will make you a better person and maybe even better than them. Social abuse occurs when your mate has a huge problem with you socializing outside of the relationship and will try to keep you from doing so by isolating you or making your feel guilty. Remember Mr. Prison Guard?

No one deserves to be abused and there is nothing you can do to warrant being treated disrespectfully. An abuser can't hide forever and they will rear their ugly head very quickly. You just need to know the signs. If you are in an abusive relationship, I know it is easier said than done, but you MUST get out. This man will never change and you could end up paying for it with your life.

Chapter Eight Playlist

The Horrible Crowes – "Ladykiller"

Mary J. Blige ft. Drake – "Mr. Wrong"

Shakira – "Did It Again"

Jo Jo – "Wrong Man For The Job"

9
Let The Hunt Begin

There are tons of good places to find men, you just have to keep your eyes open and sometimes look for them in places that you wouldn't normally look or even think about going. Just keep an open mind and remember that the man of your dreams could be checking you out when you least expect it. Mind you, the places that I am going to mention here are places that even the men I polled suggested that you look for them.

There are great places to meet men who are open to learning new things and having new experiences. Find events that really interest you so that, just in case you meet someone, you will both share a genuine interest in something. You may also want to look for professional organizations for your own line of work. How cool would it be to network and further your knowledge and career and possibly meet someone who shares the same career as you? Speaking of furthering your knowledge, if you are in school, you may find your guy sitting in the back of the classroom just waiting for you to partner with him on the next class project. If you are a true bookworm, you may make a connection in the neighborhood bookstore, library or coffeehouse. These are some of the most overlooked places to find a mate because we are so focused on what we are doing or it feels awkward to actively look for a man at these events and places. But, remember, you have to keep an open mind. If you should find a guy that you like in these places, you should have enough confidence to make eye contact more than once and smile or just go over and introduce yourself. What do you have to lose? Either you will find the man of your dreams or you will make a new friend.

Many women like to find men in church or other places of worship. Now, let's think about this for a minute. The women normally outnumber the men in church and half of them are married or sitting there with their fiancés and girlfriends. This leaves only few single men for lots of single ladies. And, let's face it, there are only so many things you can do to stand out from the other women before you are doing body shots with those little communion cups. The best way to meet a man in church is to have someone that knows him to introduce you two or just suck it up and have seat next to him and introduce yourself. Think about it, if you sit next to him, he automatically has to hold your hand during prayer time. Just make sure your hands are nice and soft. If you should be so lucky to find a man in church, kudos to you, but don't let this be the only place where you think the best men are. Truth be told, everyone in the church is not with the best of intentions, so don't be fooled by the holier than thou and super spiritual stuff. There are many devils in sheep's clothing walking around.

The grocery store is another interesting place to meet men. Just be careful what aisle you find them in. If you see a guy looking all confused in front of the hundreds of boxes of tampons, keep it moving because he has a woman at home. You can learn a lot about a man based on what's in his grocery cart. If he has beer and junk food, he may not be as interested in eating healthy as you are, but don't let that count him out. Sometimes you can use what is in his cart to start a conversation. Perhaps he has a wine or snack food that you haven't tried and you can ask him if how much he likes it. He may be trying it for the first time too and suggest you try it together. I have found myself having many conversations like what the hell you are supposed to do with tofu with some cute guy in the grocery store.

Now, let's discuss the health club. I, personally, can't stand it when men approach me in the health club because I am seriously trying to work out and I hate when something or someone disturbs my flow. This may not be the case with every woman. I will let you in a little secret though: men know when you are there to find men. It's painfully obvious when you are working out in a full face of makeup, constantly checking yourself out in the mirror and barely doing any reps. You are basically in the way for many men. The best thing to do is to tie that hair back, lose the makeup, and really get your workout on. If you are paying a monthly fee at a health club just to meet men, you should slap yourself right now. Take advantage of everything the club has to offer. If there is a guy there checking you out, he will certainly make it known. Also, don't be afraid to approach some of the men (not the male personal trainers that will flirt with you anyway) for workout tips and ask them to demonstrate. You'll learn a new move to kill a problem area and you may make a new special workout friend.

There are a few places where you should be cautious when doing your man hunting. If you are going to date someone in your immediate neighborhood, be careful. Dating someone that lives next door or in the same building can be a sticky situation if it doesn't work out. If the breakup was bad this person could do things to sabotage you with new mates they see you with, your neighbors or the places that you both frequent. Dating someone you work with can be a bad idea as well if you don't have boundaries and a clear understanding about how you will treat each other at work and how you treat each other behind closed doors. Once again, if the relationship turns sour, you could possibly be in danger of losing promotion opportunities, breaking ties with colleagues that are on your ex's side, or even losing your job. This could prove to be a fatal situation as far as your career is concerned if you are dating a superior and he doesn't want you around the office anymore once you two are done. Last, but not least, there is the nightclub. This is a total gamble because alcohol can bring out the very worst in people. Although this could be a good thing if you are trying to weed out the losers in the club, but you could be sealing your own fate if you can't hold your own liquor. Nightclubs are a breeding ground for fake, phony and pretentious people. There is also something to be said for someone who is constantly in the nightclubs as if that is the only interesting place that they know of to hang out and have fun.

Chapter Nine Playlist

Karen Kamon – "Manhunt"

Mary J. Blige – "Looking For Someone To Love Me"

Alicia Keys – "You Don't Know My Name"

Danielle Peck – "Here's To Finding a Good Man"

Nina Sky ft. Pitbull – "Turning Me On"

Beyonce – "Single Ladies"

J Boogie's Dubtronic Science – "Get it started"

10
Online Dating

In the age of rapidly advancing technology, it is no surprise that we can not only shop, video chat, and go to church online, but we can also date online. According to onlinedatingbook.org, 31% of US citizens are using dating websites. Online dating has quickly become less taboo and more of the norm. Many people don't want to go through the awkwardness of looking for a mate out in the dating scene. They just want to just cut to the chase and tell potential mates what they are all about and what they are looking for from the beginning. Online dating has become the #2 form of matchmaking in the US, scientists at the University of Rochester now report.[6]

There are online dating websites for almost any type of relationship that one may be seeking. However, choosing to find a date, a long-term relationship or even a spouse online comes with even more dilemmas than

---

[6] Searles, Rebecca. "Online Dating Now Second-Most Common Way For Couples To Meet, Study Says." *The Huffington Post.* TheHuffingtonPost.com, 7 Feb. 2012. Web. 05 Mar. 2012.

dating the old-fashioned way. You have to be really savvy and learn the whole online dating do's and don'ts. Most of what you will learn will be through trial and error.

Let me first discuss the advantages and disadvantages of online dating as well as some tips to get you started. Keep in mind that online dating is not for everyone, but don't knock it until you try it. You never know where you may find your next boyfriend.

The obvious advantage to online dating is the fact that you don't have to leave your house to scope out potential mates. You can sit at home with your laptop in your most hideous clothes and create a profile that is attractive to possible suitors. You can reveal as much or as little as possible and create a whole new life and you online. You can also search for the almost exact type of man you are looking for. You can narrow your search by race, height, weight, location, occupation and even income (be careful with the income thing; a lot of money does not make for the perfect mate) amongst other things. You get to sift through profile after profile until you find someone that you like. It is almost like "online shopping" for a mate. For most dating sites you don't even have to pay a fee, but if you do it's normally a monthly fee that is pretty affordable. You don't have to go through all of the motions of meeting someone in person for the first time ever and finding out weeks later that you have nothing in common. The one thing you have to remember that someone is also shopping for you so you have to put your best profile forward.

There are also some obvious pitfalls when it comes to online dating. There are some safety issues involved when interacting with people online. Remember the "craigslist killer?" You really need to watch your back when it comes to the strangers that you will meet until you are sure that they are not serial killers. Another issue with online dating is that the Internet has somehow become the land of make believe. People can become whomever they want on the Internet. People will lie about any and everything to be anyone but themselves and appeal to the opposite or same sex. You need to become very savvy when it comes to weeding out the posers on dating sites. People will lie about things as simple as their height, race and even where they live. Basically, the same game that men try to run on you in person can be magnified times ten on the Internet. Take a close look at the pictures that they post. Some pictures have obviously cut out a present or previous love interest. Some men are goofy enough to even include the pics with old girlfriends. Also look at the surroundings in the pictures. Is the way he is posing in the picture appropriate with the background? An inconsistency such as this could mean that the picture has been photo shopped. Who would go through that much trouble unless they have become a pro at misleading women? These are some sure ways to weed out the posers.

Online Dating Tips

For those that choose to find love online, here are some practical tips that I am sure will need:

- Be honest about who you are in your profile starting with a recent photo and not one from 15 years ago.
- Never give out your address or other personal information online. Many hackers use online dating sites to find out enough about your to steal your identity.
- Avoid telling your whole life story on your profile.
- Avoid posting your "wish list" on your profile and bashing the entire male species.

- Do not give someone that contacts you online your phone number right away.
- When in doubt, "Google" them and see what you can find out. If you find out someone is lying, it is not worth the trouble of getting to know them anyway.
- Beware of married people pretending to be single. This runs rampant on the Internet.
- If you and your new online friend decide to meet, be sure to talk to them on the phone first and have a real conversation just to make sure you really want to meet this person.
- Ask him to send you a picture via text message of him that day. This makes sure that you are talking to the same person that is supposedly online. No need to explain why you need the photo because if he likes you this should not be a problem. If he refuses, you may want to re-think meeting with him.
- Meet in a mutual place far enough from your home until you know this person better.

- Let someone know that you are going to meet this person, their name, what they look like, and where you are going.
- Drive yourself to and from the first date and so on until you feel comfortable being in this individual's vehicle with them leading the way.
- Be sure to get there earlier than you think he will so that you can watch him arrive in the parking lot. This way you know what kind of car he drives and you have a plate number. Also, if he does anything suspicious like opens the trunk to make sure he has he duct tape, you know to get the hell aware from there.
- If you can avoid drinking, do so. If not, never leave your food or drink unattended with a stranger. If you have to leave your drink or food at the table, just know that you should not continue to eat or drink when you come back. This may seem a little extreme, but I have heard some very real stories about women being drugged.
- Keep an eye on your belongings like your keys, wallet and purse.

- If you decide to be daring and meet on vacation, be sure to get your own room and rental car (if needed) and book your own flight.

All of the tips mentioned boil down to one thing and that is do not let your guard down until you truly feel like you know and trust this person. Online dating can be tricky, but you can also find a great mate if you go into it honestly, with a positive attitude and common sense.

Chapter Ten Playlist

Zapp & Roger – "Computer Love"

11
The First Date

Ok, so this is where most women go down in flames. As the old saying goes, "You only get one chance to make a first impression." This is the part where you have to prove yourself. You should have a great attitude and outlook on life, you should be feeling good about yourself inside and out and you should have a very good idea of what you are looking for in a man. You have to go into a first date with an open mind and reasonable expectations.

Of the women that I surveyed, fifty percent see a new love prospect as a potential "soul mate." This is where we go wrong ladies. If you go into every dating situation with high hopes of marriage, the picket fence and children you are setting yourself up for lots of heart break. Treat a first date as an adventure. You are getting to know someone new and you should just be in it to have a good time and find out more about them.

Just like the Fairy Godmother in Cinderella, I am going to help you get ready for your first date and walk you through some tips. After all, this is how you find out if this is a man you want to continue seeing and vice versa. Now, open your mind and pay attention.

The Perfect Outfit

First, let's make sure you are dressed appropriately. If you are not sure where your date is taking you, ask him how you should dress without giving away the surprise. This way you are not over or underdressed and you will be comfortable. The last thing you want to be worried about is how you look the whole time you are on the date because you are constantly adjusting and fixing yourself. If he says dress up and just look pretty, then do just that because chances are he is taking you somewhere nice and classy. However, if he says dress comfortable, you may want to ask how comfortable. My idea of dressing comfortable on one date was all-white Capri pants, a blouse and a three-inch heel and we were going horseback riding. Just kindly let your date know that you want to make sure that you are comfortable and you are able to have fun with him.

There are just a few things that I don't advise doing. Do not wear an overbearing perfume or one that you have not tried out yet. If he hates it, you better believe he will keep his distance when you may not want him to. Another thing you may not want to do is wear shoes that you have never worn before. If you are tiptoeing and stumbling all night this will not be a good look and you will not appear to be confident.

Mental Preparation

I usually do something that relaxes me like meditate or chant before I even go out on a date. I do this especially if my day has been stressful. You do not want to go out on a first date with a bunch of stress and BS weighing you down. Forget about what pissed you off that day, relax and get ready to have a great time.

Always remember that this new man is watching you. He is trying to find out what's wrong with you just like you are trying to find out what's wrong with him. He wants to see what makes you tick and if this will be the first date or the last. You should observe as much as you can as well. If you are a fan of chivalry, does he fit the bill? Remember that wish list of yours? You may not be able to see everything on that list in this new man, but there may be a few things you can take note of. Just remember that you may not ever meet a man that meets all of your requirements so give the guy a chance.

To Drive or Not To Drive

Should you meet him at the destination or let him pick you up? This is tricky. I really don't like to inconvenience people or make them burn a lot of expensive gas, so I don't mind meeting my date at the destination on the first date. However, that is not the only reason I would rather meet them there. Let's be honest, if the date does not go well, it's just easier to part ways and leave it at that. Who wants to make that long awkward drive home? Also, you may not want this person to know exactly where you live yet. That whole idea of a man showing up at your doorstep with flowers sounds great, but these modern times have cultivated some crazy people. I once let a guy pick me up on the first date and it didn't go so well so I politely thanked him for the ride home and I thought that was the last time I would hear from or see him again. Not! How about he showed up at my place a couple of afternoons when he knew I would be home and sleeping (I worked a night job) and wanted to "talk" as if we had just ended a long relationship. He even showed up at my job! I thought I was going to have to move out of my place that I had already lived in for four years. The last time he popped up at my house unexpectedly I had a male friend of mine waiting there with me who posed as my new boyfriend and when he saw that 6'4" linebacker body in front of him, he got the hint. So now you see why you have to be careful.

Now, there may be times when it is appropriate to let him pick you up. Perhaps you don't own a car or you are not exactly familiar with the area where he is taking you out on a date. If you choose to let him pick you up, make sure you have cab fare or someone on standby to pick you up if things don't go as planned and you prefer to part ways. In fact, you should have at least $50 to $100 on you just in case. Never go anywhere without any cash or access to cash; this is just a general rule.

Let the Date Begin!

So, now that you have met him or he has picked you up for a night of fun, it's go time! I am not going to go through what to do on every possible dating situation so let's just assume that your first date is a dinner date. Some men have learned the fine art of ordering for a woman, but don't get offended if he does not do that as this is something even the most sophisticated of men don't do. But, if he asks you what you are having, let him know; either he is trying to make a decision about his meal as well or he would like to order for you. This may seem a little awkward for some women, but if he really knows what he is doing and you let him, you are sending a message that you like the chivalry. Don't automatically assume that he is trying to control everything in a negative way. A man can show signs of being a control freak in other ways besides ordering your meal for you.

Also, be mindful of how you treat everyone from the valet to the bathroom attendant. Your date is watching you and taking notes. If you are rude or anything less than a lady, you may be sealing your fate. Remember how I checked you in Chapter One about your attitude? This is what I was preparing you for. If you are just naturally mean, nasty and rude, no man is going to put up with that (at least not the good ones) and he will not be proud to have you on his arm that night. So, go ahead and treat that waitress like she is less than human and send your plate back to the kitchen three or four times if you want to, but be prepared to go on lots of first and *last* dates. My final tips about dinner are to avoid anything you have to eat with your fingers, don't order any pasta dishes with long noodles and keep the drinking to a minimum.

Ok, so maybe I need to give the whole drinking thing a little more discussion. If you are a lightweight drinker, you should drink even less than you normally would or not at all. If one glass of wine normally puts you on your ass, then you should probably just drink half a glass or some good ole iced tea. If you are one that can hold your liquor pretty well, you should still drink less than you would normally drink. The whole point is to not get wasted or even tipsy. Granted you will feel any alcohol you drink, but as soon as you feel it, stop drinking. You don't want to make any bad decisions or make a bad impression. The impression you make may be that you have a drinking problem or just don't know when to say no and are unaware of your personal limits. This can send all types of assumptions through a man's mind about your personal values. As far as decisions are concerned, no woman wants to be the subject of a story that a man tells his friends the next day about the girl who he went out on a date with and got so wasted that she...(you fill in the blanks). Don't be THAT girl.

The Conversation

So, now that you are on this date and eating, what else do you do? Get to know this guy. Talk! Now, don't get too carried away with the whole talking thing. What I mean by talk is have a conversation where you both have almost an equal amount of words coming out of your mouths. I am saying it like this because women love to talk. I know I do. So, here is what you are going to do: you are going to shut up and listen. I know I seem really mean, but this is the only way some of you will really sit up and pay attention.

Men love to talk about themselves, that is, if you let them. This is your chance to flip it on him and make him do most of the talking so that you can find out as much as you need to know about him. Ask him about his job, his family, what he likes to do for fun, where he likes to travel, his favorite band, or even his thoughts on a current event. Now when I say current events, I do not mean political or religious. A good example could be all the new condo developments in your city, a new business chain opening in your region or even some annual event coming to your city. You have to be very skilled to talk politics and religion without getting into conflict. If you have this skill and really want to feel him out, go for it, but you have been warned. I am not saying that you should never talk about these two subjects with him, but it is not a good idea for a first date conversation.

You may be on a first date with someone is shy or not very forthcoming with information giving short answers. This is where you must quickly develop the gift of gab without gabbing too much. Listen to his answers and use what he says to ask another question to get deeper into the subject. If he is only giving you one word answers throughout the night, this is a red flag that he may not be into you or this may not be the guy for you. Pay attention.

You also don't want to talk about prior relationships, marriage, money or gossip. Lots of times these subjects come up when a woman has lost control of the conversation. As soon as you allow him to start asking a series of questions, you will answer not only those questions but even some he didn't ask. Men love it when you talk about all these things because they can make some quick decisions about you on the first date and avoid spending any more time with you if they don't like what they hear. If you start talking about a series of bad relationships, that fact that you want to get married like yesterday and you are bad with money, this is great for a man. He knows everything he needs to know and you have possibly crossed your name off the list. I am not saying that you should never tell him about your thoughts on marriage or money management, but you still need to keep it light for the first date.

The hard and fast rule that you must follow in order to be respectful is to turn off your cell phone or at least put it away and do not bring it out during the date. I understand you may have to check on your kids or your job may call so if that is the case, just excuse yourself and go the restroom and make or take your call. If you notice that he keeps taking his phone out, call him on it, but in a clever way. You could say something like, "You sure are mister popular." Either he will put his phone away or he may even let you know that he is on call for work or checking on his own kids. Either way, you have to make it known that you demand respect if you are respecting him. Honestly, the only time I take my phone out on a date is when there is something I want to show my date or we are at an event that just has to be photographed or caught on video. I never text or make phone calls unless it is urgent and I am very apologetic when I have to pull that phone out.

Another rule you should follow is DO NOT dumb yourself down. By this I mean don't just throw all of those advanced degrees, intellect and hard-core common sense out of the window to appeal to this man. It's no secret that men love to have their egos stroked, hell we all do, but you don't have to appear to be less intelligent to make him feel good about himself. This sometimes comes into play when a woman with lots of formal education dates a man who is successful or making a come up but may not have the same level of education. In my lifetime I have dated some very successful men who did not go past high school or maybe they went to trade school or learned on the job. What's interesting is I learned more from them than they learned from me about business and the ways of the world. In turn, they would ask me for advice based on my book smarts and I was always happy to show them how smart I was and they appreciated my intelligence. On the flip side, I have also dated very nice blue-collar men who may not have been as educated as I or even as polished. However, I never felt the need to "come down to their level" to speak to them or relate to them. I had just as much respect for them as I did the white-collar man because they had interesting stories to tell as well.

The only thing that would get on my nerves is a man who made me feel like I was not allowed to do or say anything that made me appear to be smarter than he was. There would be smart little remarks like, "Is that all they teach you in college?" This is a sure sign that you are dealing with an insecure prick and it will only get worse.

While you are not dumbing yourself down, be sure not to pretend to be more intelligent than you actually are. I know that seems crazy, but pay attention. I once went out on a date with a guy who was talking about a subject that was totally foreign to me. I may read a lot and try my best to learn something new every chance I get, but I doubt that I will ever be a contestant on Jeopardy. The whole time this guy was talking, I was nodding my head and agreeing and just following his lead. That is, until he asked me a question. I quickly changed the subject, but it was clear that I had no idea what he was talking about. The lesson in this is if you don't know, just ask. Men love to talk about themselves, but they also like to talk about the things that interest them just like you do. So sit there and listen and if you get lost in the conversation, stop him and ask questions. If you just sit there and nod your head like a little puppet, you will lose his respect once he finds out you are clueless.

So, now that you made it through that first date made it home safely, in your own car or his, what do you do? If you did not thank him for a nice evening, you better be racing to pull that phone out to text him to say thank you. This man probably could have taken someone else out that night, but he chose you so just a small thank you for his time and I guarantee he will also thank you for your time. If your dance card is full, you certainly could have been spending the evening with someone else as well.

A man, who is truly interested in going beyond the first date with you, will more than likely initiate the next contact. But, don't you dare wait by the phone and I know you won't because you have a life to live and you no longer immediately think of every man as a potential husband. However, do keep in mind that men can be shy too and not sure how to make the first move when they are into a woman and not sure how to let her know he is interested.

Wait about two days and send him a text or email asking him how he is doing and if he would like to "hang out" again soon. If he responds, he responds. If he doesn't, he doesn't. I use the phrase "hang out" because it comes across as you being more carefree and makes him more comfortable asking you out again. If it doesn't go any further, you had a great night and will have many more with other great guys or that special one. Don't sweat it.

If he doesn't call back, there may be reasons for this such as:

- You broke the rules and talked about marriage and practically had the man walking down the aisle and picking out paint for a nursery
- You didn't show much interest such as constantly pulling your phone out or obviously being distracted
- You may have been a pawn in his game while he is playing the field; kind of like how you may be taking boyfriend applications at this time

- You weren't on your best behavior i.e. rude, got a little too tipsy, or possibly insulted or embarrassed him in some way
- Some men are cowards and don't have the nerve to tell you they aren't into you so they avoid calling you

Let's say he calls back and I know he will because you are fabulous and put your best foot forward. If he asks you out on another date, make sure you are fitting him into your schedule. Remember, you don't cancel anything you have going on if it is not necessary. Many women feel like if they don't accept his offer of a second date or any date on his terms, he is going to take the offer off of the table. This is what a true asshole may do, but not a man who is into you. A man who is into you will work with your schedule and respect and appreciate the fact that you have a life beyond him. But, don't make him wait just for the sake of making him wait. If you have nothing going on during the time he wants to see you, then accept the date. Dating should be fun, but it should not be a game that you play to one-up a man.

Chapter Eleven Playlist

Maxwell – "Get To Know Ya"

J-Boogie – "Get It Started"

Taylor Swift – "Enchanted"

Lloyd ft. 50 Cent – "Let's Get It In"

Sade – "Kiss of Life"

Tamia – "So Into You"

Michael Buble' – "Haven't Met You Yet"

Prince – "Strollin'"

Blink 182 – "First Date"

Cranberries – "Kiss Me"

Elle Varner – "Refill"

12
Should You Or Shouldn't You

Before we move on, we have to back up to that first date and answer and age-old question: Is it okay to have sex on the first date? My fast and short answer to that question is: **No!**

Now, don't go tucking your tail between your legs because you feel ashamed of something you may have done. You did it, it's done and now you move on. Now, you will learn how to handle the situation when it comes up again. And there is a good chance that it will. I was actually surprised when many of the women that I surveyed said they had sex on the first date and the relationships lasted for more than a year; some lasted for multiple years and even turned into marriage. But, keep in mind that those relationships may be in the minority and other things may have factored into their longevity. For example, they may have been known each other for quite a while before dating and felt comfortable enough to get physical.

Let's be honest, many women know if they are going to sleep with a man before the first date even ends. It's just a matter of when you decide to give up the goodies. If men knew that they had already won the prize without actually getting it, they would act a whole lot different. I'm talking about these men will be on their best behavior and damn near walk over hot coals in their bare feet for you. Unfortunately, none of us will ever say on the first date, "So, I just want to let you know that I have every intention of sleeping with you, but I am just waiting on the right moment when I am ready." So the poor guy is left wondering while we are agonizing on how soon is too soon and how long we should make him wait.

There have been many books written that tell women how long they should wait. Some books have the nerve to tell us exactly how many days, weeks, months and years we should wait. Now I am not knocking this type of advice because there is a lot of logic behind it, but a woman knows when she is ready. Only you know when it's the right time for you, but make sure it is truly the right time. My best advice is to only share yourself with a man who knows your worth, who has expressed that he is "all in" with you and wants an exclusive relationship, and respects you.

You should never have sex with a man on the first date or anytime because you feel obligated after he has done something for you. If he only did something nice for you to get you in the sack, he's hardly a man that deserves what you have to offer. You should also avoid putting yourself in a position that could lead to sex such as having a first date at either one of your houses. Cuddling turns into kissing, kissing turns into "touching", "touching" turns into undressing and undressing turns into sex.

I think the biggest fear that women have is that if we sleep with the guy on the first date, will he lose respect for us or not even want to have anything to do with us afterwards. Well ladies, there is some reason to worry and then, surprisingly, there are some reasons not to worry. I had numerous conversations with men on this topic.

The majority of the men revealed that they would not think any less of a woman who had sex on the first date. For these men, it is more about how the woman approaches the situation. If she wants to just skip desert and rush to his place and get in the sack, this will give him pause. Perhaps not enough pause not to do the deed with her anyway, but enough to not want to form a real relationship with this woman. Many men said that a woman that takes this approach will have them wondering if this is a normal practice for her. So, if you are truly not into sex on the first date and you just happen to indulge, your man may not think any less of you if he can see that you are not a "pro" at it. This still seems a little risky, but if it happens just hope and pray that he doesn't think you are just a woman in heat that gives it up on the first date. You have been educated and warned now.

Guys tend to be more chivalrous to women they respect. They tend to want to really show their woman that they are worthy of the prize and will not take it for granted when they get it. Men will go out of their way to let you know that you will be safe and secure in their hands and that they are more than worthy of becoming one with you. I know this all sounds very mushy, but you need to understand how important it is to value your self-worth, which will make you put an even higher value on what is between your legs. In other words, if you wouldn't let this man have a sip of your drink through your straw, how can you possibly have sex with him? I know that is a weird analogy, but I have seen couples who will not share a dessert, but will do some porn star level acts between the sheets. Now how does that make any sense?

The biggest fear that we have is that he will get what he wants and then we will never hear from him again or he will not treat us as well as he did before the sex. This is very much possible which is why you really have to be as good of a judge of character as you possibly can. My rule of thumb if you are on the fence about having sex with a man on the first date or very early in the relationship is to think about if this is a man you would want to have children with and deal with for the next 18 years. If that's not some hardcore reality for you, then I don't know what is.

Chapter Twelve Playlist

Liz Phair – "Fuck and Run"

Jamie Foxx – "Can I Take You Home"

Enrique Iglesias – "One Night Stand"

Alicia Keys – "Un-thinkable (I'm Ready)"

Monica – "The First Night"

Janis Joplin – "One Night Stand"

Marsha Ambrosius – "With You"

Tweet ft. Missy Elliot – "Turn Da Lights Off"

Keri Hilson ft. Chris Brown – "One Night Stand"

Chris Brown – "No Bull"

Sleepy Brown ft. Outkast – "I Can't Wait"

13
Be The Prey

Men are hunters by nature. They love to go out and hunt their prey, catch it and bring it back for all the other men to see. In relationships, consider yourself the prey. From day one, this man's goal is to impress you and make you his. Do not take this away from him. You basically have to learn how to play hard to get without coming off as though you are playing games. It's quite the balancing act.

You must remain a mystery to him as long as you can. A man does not need to know your whole life story within a month of the first date. He should be on a need to know basis. The key is to make him keep wanting to know more about you. He needs to feel intrigued by you. Once a man knows everything about you, you feel like there is nothing keeping his interest. I have dated people who were still finding out something new about me even after dating for a couple of years. What's funny is that I didn't purposely hold the information back; it just never came up and was not pertinent to the relationship. If a man is truly interested in you, he will be dying to know more about you. You have to give him a reason to want to know more. Be that mystery woman that he loves.

You don't need to call or text your man every time you think of him or miss him. This is very hard to do once you have bonded with a man, but try your best. It's great if your man makes you have random thoughts about him throughout the day, but he doesn't need to know it every time you do. He will start to think that you have nothing else going on or to think about.

It's fine to call or text your man when you want to talk, but just make sure you are not always the one to initiate every conversation. Let him call you. However, if you don't call your man for a week because you really have nothing important to say and he doesn't call you either, that is a red flag. A man that is into you will at least send up a smoke signal once a day even if he is super busy to let you know you were on his mind at some point. People make time for what they want to make time for and if he can't call you for a week and is capable of doing so, perhaps you need to rethink your relationship with him.

Although you may always have great ideas for dates, let him come up with the plans for the evening as much as possible. Men like to be in charge and if you are always dictating what you will do as a couple, this could make him feel as though you are a bit controlling. The best way to help him to make plans that you will both enjoy is make sure he is aware of your likes and dislikes. For example, if he knows you can't swim, he won't be taking you out scuba diving. I once dated a guy who either kept forgetting or didn't care that I have severe (pretty much deadly) allergies to fresh water fish and peanuts. He kept suggesting that we go to sushi restaurants. It was not only annoying, but I felt disrespected because it showed me that he didn't listen to me or even try to pay attention to details.

If you want to keep that man interested, you need to let him meet you halfway when it comes to running the relationship. In fact, you may even want to let him meet you more than halfway. Make him work for your time, but not too hard as you may make him want to find a woman that is a little more available.

Chapter Thirteen Playlist

Peter Frampton – "Baby I Love Your Way"

Mario – "Let Me Love You"

R. Kelly – "Love Letter"

Tyrese – "Sweet Lady"

Melanie Fiona – "Give It To Me"

Avant ft. Keke Wyatt – "You and I"

14
The Essentials

Without trust and respect in a relationship, you are doomed. These two things are the foundation of your relationship. I am amazed sometimes at how people conduct themselves in relationships these days. Whatever happened to chivalry and being ladies and just valuing the person you are with?

Trust is one of the biggest issues in relationships. My own rule is that I will give a man the rope and he must decide if he will tie it in a pretty bow and give it back to me or hang himself. I don't try to keep my man on lockdown. I want him to go out with his friends and hang out without me calling his phone every half hour for updates. I have never been the type to have a fit whenever my man wanted his "me" time. Why? Well, isn't it obvious? I don't want my man trippin' when I want my "me" time alone or with my friends. In fact, the only time I have ever had a problem with my man going out is when an ex had a habit of going out three or four times a week and staying out way past a time that I thought was acceptable to come stepping back in the house. If I did that, he would have had a stone cold bitch fest on me. So let's discuss trust for a little bit.

A person will only do what you allow them to get away with. This holds true in any type of relationship from business to personal. You have to let your man know up front what you will and will not accept and be firm. This does not mean that you sit him down and go over the rules with him as if he is at his first day of boot camp. The easiest way to do this is to first ask him what he wants in a woman and listen carefully. Be sure that you can live up to those wants if they are reasonable. Then, it's your turn. When I tell a man what I am looking for, the first thing that comes out of my mouth is, "He must be respectful." A real man will know exactly what you mean. A man who may not be comfortable or is not sure if he can live up to your needs will start to squirm in his seat a little because you have to say it with the most serious look on your face as possible. This lets him know there are no exceptions to this rule. A man who is respectful will more than likely be trustworthy. He knows that you are not going to let him play any games with you. You have given him the rope and now you just watch and see what he does with it. However, some women will help the man tie his own noose.

There are a lot of women that only trust their men as long as they are standing next to them and, even then, they are on their ass. They have a fit if they even *think* their man just looked at the pretty girl that just walked in the room. The man is in a relationship with you, but this doesn't mean that all of a sudden he is blind. They are going to look. It should only be a problem if he keeps glancing over or even starts to stare. Just don't cause a scene and be sure to address it as soon as possible because men will get amnesia as soon as you get home. Just let him know that it made you feel a certain type of way when he did it and leave it up to him to correct it and make sure it never happens again. A man that is into you is not going to do anything that makes you feel uncomfortable. This takes care of things he may do in your presence, but what about when you are not around.

Let's go ahead address the mighty Internet and it's social networking demon spawn. That may have been a little dramatic for a description, but social networks can indeed be the "devil" and have caused the rifts and break ups of many relationships. One thing we have to remember is that it is social networking and it is meant to connect people from all over the world who may never get to meet in person but may share a special interest that connects them on the web. Where we go wrong is when we are constantly monitoring our mate's activities on these websites. If you are watching his every move, of course it will seem that his is "liking" too many other women's pictures and statuses. You have to remember that hitting the like button does not mean that he wants to meet up with that woman or has something going on with her. Most people absent-mindedly hit like because it is just a habit or maybe they feel obligated to "like" because that person hit "like." Don't read too much into this.

On the flip side, make sure that you are not doing things that make your man uncomfortable. One thing I notice is many women will allow so-called male "friends" to make very suggestive comments on their pictures. Sometimes these men know the woman is in a relationship and they don't care and sometimes they have no idea. They probably have no idea because the women has somehow let it slip her mind to remind these fellas that she is in a relationship. Personally, if I am in a relationship, I rarely even post a clue that I am involved because I just don't want people in my business and the men I date are rarely into social networking or barely online. However, if you know your man can see your posts and the comments and "likes" that are posted, it is up to you to do damage control even before the damage happens. If you don't, be prepared to do some explaining if there is always one, two or even a handful of guys *always* making suggestive comments about your photos. If he mentions it, it bothers him and you need to make sure that it does not continue to happen. Now, back to your man and his online activities.

Oh and insisting that you both acknowledge that you are in a relationship on these sites is not going to do much either. A no good woman will not care that you are in his profile picture or that his status says "in a relationship" just like a scandalous woman on the street that sees a man holding hands with his woman and still wants to take him.

Your man may not feed into it, but just know that some chicks just don't care. And for goodness sakes, please don't be *that* chick. You know the chick who goes and looks at the profile of every woman that "likes" or "comments" on her man's picture or status or even makes sure that she puts her two cents in on every comment and picture her man posts just to make her presence known. I remember when I would sometimes comment on a guy's photos that I had never even met in person and his wife would always have to refer to my comment when making her own and then top it off with, "I love you baby." I got a good chuckle out of this because I had never met this man, didn't find him the least bit attractive, but I liked the pictures that he posted because he was a photographer. Sometimes I would just comment just to make her react and amuse myself. Don't be the chick getting laughed at because folks know that you are insecure. Honestly, going on your man's profiles to constantly check up on him is just as bad as snooping.

Yes, snooping! Now we can discuss the other elephant in the room. Women are nosey. Given the opportunity we will poke our nose all in someone's business and it is very tempting when you are in a relationship. You want to know all of his little secrets and if he is doing anything behind your back. The snooping stops after the first date. You only get a pass to do a web search on him before you go out with him for safety reasons. After that first date, if you want to know something you will just have to ask. Now I know you are now twisting your lips in doubt thinking that if you ask there is a good chance that he will lie. This is true, but once you get to know this man, you will know when he is not being totally honest with you. Simply put, there is no reason for you to go through his phone or his personal belongings because it is wrong and you sure in the hell wouldn't want him to do it to you. Usually, if a woman feels the need to go snooping through her man's things, she already knows that he is up to no good and is only seeking confirmation. Seek and you shall find and you may not like what you find so just ask him what you want to know.

You should also know that constantly asking a man these probing questions will more than likely drive him insane if he is not out there doing you wrong. The fastest way to lose your man is to accuse him of cheating every other day. When a man is made to feel that any little thing he does that seems suspicious is going to set his woman off into a finger-pointing frenzy, he will run. Who wants to feel like they are always walking on eggshells around someone? Sure, there are some men who are prone to cheat or those who, given the opportunity, will cheat. However, if you are constantly accusing an innocent man you could even drive him to fulfill your prophecy. So, stand back and let him show you who he is. A cheater will soon be caught.

Basically, you have to respect each other's expectations and limits. If you truly feel like you cannot trust someone, then it is probably not a good idea to be in a relationship with that person. Constantly worrying about the integrity of your relationship is certainly not going to make you happy.

Chapter Fourteen Playlist

Etta James – "Trust In Me"

Black Eyes Peas – "Shut Up"

Amerie ft. Fabolous – "More Than Love"

Melanie Fiona – "4 am"

Keyshia Cole ft. Monica – "Trust"

Carrie Underwood – "Before He Cheats"

Miami Sound Machine – "Uh Oh"

Phenomenal 1 ft. Nycee – "Secret Agent"

Sade – "Nothing Can Come Between Us"

Beyonce' – "Ring The Alarm"

The Police – "Every Breath You Take"

Sonny Boy Williamson – "Your Funeral My Trial"

The Human League – "Don't You Want Me"

Deniece Williams – "Silly"

Al Green – "Love and Happiness"

Jazmine Sullivan – "Bust The Windows"

Billie Holiday – "I'm A Fool To Want You"

15
He Loves You/He Loves You Not

First, I am going to tell you all about the signs that man is into you and may even love you or be in love with you. And yes, I asked men what it was that they did or do to show a woman that they love her. One thing that I noticed is that the men rarely said that they actually say, "I love you." This can be very frustrating for women because many of us need to hear those three words. But, suck it up ladies because your man may rarely say those words and it may take him a while to say them.

What men *will* do is go out of their way to show us how much they care for and love us. So let me just go ahead and ease your minds and let you know how these men we love operate.

He can't take his eyes off of you. I know this may seem a little misleading because a man that is constantly eyeing you could just be lusting after you. However, there is a look that a man can give you that will give you real butterflies. It's a look that says I love every word that is coming out of your mouth. In fact, your man will have no problem looking directly into your eyes when you speak and there is something about those eyes locking that can tell you all you need to know.

He is interested in everything about you and remembers the smallest details. This may seem a little strange but it bothers me when I tell a man that I am allergic to peanuts and he is still offering and suggesting food with peanuts to me after we have been on several dates. I feel like if I have taken the time out to learn what makes him tick, his likes and dislikes, then he should do the same. A man that wants to please you will want to know exactly how to do so and will be very attentive when you tell him what you are all about and passionate about. He'll then use that information to please you in any way he can.

He's there for the good and bad times. A true test of a man who is all in is if he can handle you at your worst. This doesn't mean that he perseveres through a major temper tantrum. It means that he is there for you when are facing a challenge or even a major crisis. He answers the phone and sits there and listens, he comes to your aid, and he may even try to help you if possible. A man who disappears when you need him the most is not all that into you and you should take note of it. A real man will be there to hold you up when you feel like you are falling and will never let you hit the ground.

He supports your decisions and dreams. Women have no problem being their man's biggest cheerleader. However, there are times when we need someone in our corner cheering us on and giving us encouragement. A good man will support all the good that you want to happen in your life. He will be just as excited as you are when good things happen in your life. In fact, he may do things that will help you along with your dreams like buy you a new computer to help you manage your business, buy you a new camera to support your photography business or even help you out with your tuition even if you don't really need these things. Even if he doesn't buy you "things" to help you along, just having that man in your corner and encouraging you along the way is enough so be sure you let him know how much you appreciate it every step of the way. A good man that cares about you will also let you know when you are making poor decisions. No one likes to be told that they are doing or about to do something wrong or bad for them, but when it comes from the mouth of a man that loves you, you should really listen.

He is okay with your interests outside of the relationship and even encourages it. There is nothing worse than a man that has a hissy fit every time you want to go out and pursue one of your hobbies or interests without him. His little fit is well understood if you are constantly putting these habits before him and never compromise, but he has to understand that your "me time" is important. In fact, this may be one of those little red flags that should alert you to what could be a controlling man. Sit up and pay attention. He should be okay with you doing things solo or with friends without him being attached to your hip and you should be okay with him doing the same.

He makes you feel important. Let's be clear, in these ultra-modern times, folks are super busy. People have to stay one up on their careers and anything else in their life that ensures their place in society. However, people also make time for what they want to make time for. By this I mean, your man will always make time for you and, if he can't, you will know why. It is up to you to understand when he is unable to pick up the phone because he is in a meeting. However, he also has the responsibility of letting you know when it's just not a good time because he is handling his business and not just ignore you. Nothing drives us up the wall more than a man who doesn't answer a call or text message for hours or even a day or two when we are always responsive. Speaking of text messages, this is the technology that allows your man to quickly alert you to the fact that he is tied up so there is no excuse for unanswered communication for ridiculously long periods of time. A man who is totally into you will not ignore your calls and will respond as quickly as he can. He will also initiate the contact as much as you do. If you find yourself constantly initiating contact between the two of you, because if you don't you two may never talk, then perhaps you need to fall back and be careful before you invest anymore time or unanswered phone calls into this man.

Another way a man can make you feel important is by making sure you are not always last on his list. First, let's keep it real and realize that you may not always be first if you are at girlfriend status. If he has children, just know that they will *always* come first. Some men will try to find a way to involve you with their children so you understand how much you and they mean to him, but realize that this is a huge step for men. However, there will be times when he is not choosing between you and his children or other members of his family and he should be choosing you. If you constantly have to fight to be high on this man's list of priorities, this may not be a battle that you want to engage in. There is no better self-esteem killer than feeling like you are always the last person whose needs your man thinks about. For your part, you must also remember when it is best to put your man first and let him know that you care about his feelings and needs.

He starts sharing his plans for the future and includes you. Please notice that *he* starts sharing first. This is very important. You have to tread lightly when thinking about a possible future with your man. Many men have told me that women should not start leaving their toothbrush at a man's house until he asks you to. In fact, wait until he actually buys you a toothbrush to keep at his house. Now, this is only figurative, but it is very important. A man who wants you to be in his life for a while, and maybe even forever, will flat out tell you or make it pretty damn obvious. He will encourage you to leave things at his house and make yourself comfortable. It's a good idea to let him bring up marriage, kids and the future first.   There is no rule saying that you can't quiz him a little and see where his mind is as far as you are concerned, but I don't advise asking, "So, when are you going to introduce me to your family, pop the question and start picking out china patterns?"   The key here is not to scare him off, but also don't wait for an unreasonable amount of time for him to talk about a future with you.   How much time is considered unreasonable? Only you can answer that question. The answer depends on where you are in your own life and what you have planned for yourself. If you want to see a real commitment after a year, then you need to start probing him a little. If you are fine waiting more than a year because you have things going on in your life that you need to work on, then that is fine too. The point is time waits for no one and you can't waste your time on a man who is stagnant in the relationship. You could be out there having fun dating other men.

Probably the biggest sign that this man is really feeling you is when he brings you into his world and introduces you to his family and friends. It's a safe bet that if he brings you home to mama, you are in there! If he also brings you to events where all of his closest friends are present, you have now become that woman that he wants to show off to all his friends and he is proud to have you on his arm. He may even invite you to work-related events. Just make sure that while you are meeting mama, his friends and his boss that he introduces you as more than a friend. If you are his *friend* there is definitely, in football terms, a flag on the play. You need to dial it back and also stop having sex with him immediately if you are having sex because you don't have sex with your *friends*. In fact, you should know that you are the *girlfriend* before you even have sex with him anyway. It is not considered playing games if you have to do this because you have made a fatal mistake and you *must* correct it for the sake of your dignity, which is more important than anything.

So now, we have come to the shit that will blow your mind. There are some men out there that will do all of the above and have no more love for you than they did for the last meal they ate. These men want what I call "the girlfriend experience." It's also a common term among escorts. They want all of the benefits of having a woman in their life without actually acknowledging that woman as their girlfriend or even their significant other. The girlfriend experience is one step up from being friends with benefits. Imagine giving a starving homeless person a nice place to live and plenty of food to eat for a year and then abruptly kicking them back out on the streets. This is the equivalent of what the girlfriend experience will do to you. You are sold a dream. What's crazy is you may actually prefer being friends with benefits because at least you know from the beginning where you stand and there are no real expectations between you two.

The girlfriend experience has been known to leave a trail of hurt after it runs through a woman's life. Men that prefer this type of arrangement typically are fresh out of a relationship, recently (or not so recently) divorced, or just nowhere near being ready for a real committed relationship. They want a woman to keep their bed warm when they want sex and will even lay there and cuddle with you afterward. They want someone to go to movies, dinner and other events with them so they don't have to go alone. They want someone on their arm when they are around their friends who have wives and girlfriends. They also want someone to bring around their family to quiet them and stop them from asking if and when they will ever settle down. What these men should be looking for is an escort. They show up, fulfill his needs, and leave and there are no strings attached. Unfortunately, these men are not aware that when they awaken the love inside a woman, they can't just turn it off. A man who is looking for the girlfriend experience is only looking for a placeholder to satisfy his own needs until he gets bored with that woman or finds the woman that he really wants. Nothing hurts more than being with a man, giving him your all, he pulls a disappearing act and then you find out he has found someone new or is even getting married.

I have been through it a couple of times. However, I have finally learned to be a little stingy with my love and efforts in a relationship until I know that man's intentions. It's quite awful that there are men that will play on our feelings, but we can't put it all on them. It's up to us to set certain expectations from the beginning and make sure the man is meeting them.

You need to recognize the signs quickly if you think you may be providing a girlfriend experience for a man. If you ask this man where the relationship is going (you really shouldn't have to ask this if he is into you) and he gives you some vague answer all I have to say is, "Run, girl, run!" If he can't even tell you straight up how he feels about you or his plans with you, then beware that you may be a pawn in his game. The biggest clue is that he does all those things above that suggest that he is into you and then he stops cold turkey. This means that he has finished playing with you because you are now too close and he needs to push you away or he has moved on to another woman. Another clue is if he lacks consistency. This means that he does all the things that a boyfriend does sporadically. A man who is sporadic with his affection is only affectionate when it serves his purposes and none of yours. In fact, you should realize this very quickly because the affection will come out of nowhere when he has barely touched you for days, weeks or longer. A man that wants a loyal woman will be consistent because he realizes that this is high on our list of needs as the emotional creatures that we are. A man who is only looking for a plaything or toy will fail to realize that women have feelings, dreams and desires.

Finding out that you were only the girlfriend experience will pretty much make you feel the lowest of lows, but it is important that you learn from this experience and make sure that it never repeats itself. Should you steer clear of men fresh out of relationships or divorced men? Not necessarily. But, you should tread lightly and not give as much of yourself until you know where you stand with this man and his intentions with you. This means that you don't do anything that a wife or even a girlfriend would do until you know for sure that you are in an exclusive relationship with him. Never give a man more than he is willing to give you. By this, I don't mean gifts. I mean all of the things that feed your heart.

Chapter Fifteen Playlist

Luke James – "I.O.U."

Miguel – "Adorn"

Ohio Players – "Heaven Must Be Like This"

Aerosmith – "I Don't Want To Miss A Thing"

Stevie Wonder – "As"

Savage Garden – "Truly Madly Deeply"

Chris Young – "You"

Brian Adams – "(Everything I Do) I Do It For You"

Slique – "Addicted"

DeBarge – "I Like It"

Prince – "Call My Name"

Dave Hollister – "One Woman Man"

For those who have been "The Girlfriend Experience":

K. Michelle – "Sometimes"

Jazmine Sullivan – "Holding you down (Goin' in Circles)"

16
Calling it Quits

More women that I surveyed have experienced a bad breakup versus the men. Why is this? Is it because men just don't give a damn once the relationship is over? Not at all. Men can feel the same amount of hurt as a woman if the relationship was truly a loss to him. The difference between men and woman is that men departmentalize things and how they handle them. They have a separate space for everything in their lives such as career, family, hobbies and love. If the love department is not working, they quickly shift to another department. Unfortunately, women don't have departments. We have been groomed to be able to deal with all of our life issues all at once and can't just shove off one to focus on another.

Face it, a break up can break you completely down if you were truly in love with that person. You will feel like your heart has been ripped out of your chest and someone has punched you in the stomach at the same time. You may feel as though you can't go on without that person because they had become such a big part of your life. You are dreading the fact that your ex will find someone else and be just as happy, if not happier, with this new person. Worst of all, you feel like you will never find someone as good as your ex. All of these feelings are perfectly normal, but you will have to learn how to deal with these feelings and then move on with your life. You will want to cry it out, but you can't cry forever. I know this is a lot easier said than done.

What I find interesting is that more of the women I surveyed admitted that they were confused about the breakup than the men. Many times, if the man ends the relationship, he may give the woman a reason for breaking things off that is not all that true. Sometimes they do so because giving you the real reason may cause a fight that will result in a messy breakup. In fact, this is the biggest reason for them to lie about it.

Another reason may be that there is something personal about you that they just can't bring themselves to say that they are just not attracted to. This could be anything from your sudden weight gain to your lack of ambition. The man simply doesn't want to leave you in tears. Still, the simplest reason for the breakup may be that he has found someone else and is too much of a coward to tell you. As women, we want the same feedback from our men that we want from our boss during a performance review. The problem is that once you have been fired, what's the point in continuing to tell you what you are doing wrong if you could have made changes early on. Every now and then, while you are still in the relationship and all is well, stop and ask your mate how he thinks things are going and if there is anything he thinks may be lacking in the relationship. Once the relationship is over, you will not be able to do this. The only time I have ever been able to find out what really caused a breakup (that is, if I was the one that got dumped) is years later when everything was water under the bridge and we had both moved on.

Instead of looking for closure and reason from your ex, you have to concentrate on getting back on the path of being happily single and starting over. I know it sucks to be back out there again searching but such is life and you now have the tools to be able to do it better. You should never consider a breakup as a failure, but as a lesson. Each new relationship teaches you more about yourself, love, men and people in general.

You need to shake it off and regroup before you get back out there and date again. This means that you need to make sure the anger, hurt, anxiety, depression and anything else you are feeling has subsided before you go back out on the dating scene. If you don't let all of these feelings pass, the next man will fall victim to all of these feelings and you may lose a good man over it.

The first thing you may want to do is gather a support group of your closest friends that you can be honest with about your feelings. The purpose of the support group is not to have "bash your ex" sessions, but to surround yourself with people who you know care about you and will not judge you for the way you are feeling. Also, make sure that when you are with those who are helping to counsel you that it is not always about you being sad. You can't be a "downer" every time you are with your friends because they will start to run the other way when they see you coming. This may sound bad, but you will have to use these people as distractions to keep your mind off of your ex. Just make sure you are there to return the favor when your friends need your support for the same reason. Do all of the things that you would normally do with your friends and try your best not to discuss your ex. You will be surprised how if you consciously refrain from thinking about or mentioning your ex how easy it is to do so unconsciously after a while.

One thing that may help you get over your ex quickly is by getting rid of all of those sentimental mementos, within reason of course. By mementos, I am referring to cards, flowers pressed into books, love letters, etc.; those things that bring up memories of you two together. Constantly having these things in your face will make it very hard to get over him. What about expensive gifts like jewelry, gadgets or even cars? This can be tricky. It really depends on the nature of your relationship or even if he is requesting that certain items (the car) be returned to him. Personally, I keep gifts because it is just rude to get rid of them even though I may not really wear or use them anymore. It all depends on the emotions and feelings that are attached to that "thing". At any rate, even though you may want to go all *Waiting To Exhale* on him, burn everything and send him the ashes, think before you act. I would also advise you to wait and make sure that there is no chance for you to reconcile the relationship. It would be a tough conversation trying to explain what happened to that life-sized teddy bear that once sat in the corner of your bedroom that he won at a carnival if you get back together.

Remember the part where I discussed "Getting a Life?" This is why that is so important. If you had interests and a life beyond your relationship, you should have plenty of things to do to keep you busy. Life must go on and if you don't have anything to keep you occupied, you have to get out of the house and try anything. You should be hanging out at your favorite coffee shop reading, attending a class to learn a new hobby, and hanging out with your friends. One thing that seems to help many women get over an ex is changing something about themselves. Perhaps a new hair color, a few new outfits to change up your style or even a day at the spa to rejuvenate your body. If you can do so, go on a vacation either by yourself or with friends. These are all things that you can do that will help you to move on and it should all be very easy since you were sure to keep your own life going while being part of a couple.

Once, you feel up to it and can go an entire week without thinking about your ex, go on some casual light-hearted dates and be clear with the guy that you are just meeting new people and having fun. No need to have some poor guy giving you the "boyfriend experience" if you are not planning on getting into a relationship with him. Just keep it light and have fun until you are able to dive into a new relationship without bringing any baggage from your old relationship. Only you know when you are ready. I once held out from getting into any relationships for a whole year after a breakup. I knew I just needed to work on me for a while and also work on accomplishing some personal goals. Your relationship may have been holding you back and the breakup is an opportunity to see what you may have been missing.

Once you have picked yourself up and dusted off, get back out there and try again. You now have all of the tools and confidence you need to let any man know how great you are and why he should be with you. So, go out there and be sexy, be vibrant, and most of all, be happy!

Chapter Sixteen Playlist

Mary J. Blige – "Enough Cryin'"
Adele – "Rolling In The Deep"
Jazmine Sullivan – "10 Seconds"
Chrisette Michele – "Epiphany (I'm Leaving)"
Leona Lewis – "Better In Time"
Whitney Houston – "I will Always Love You"
K. Michelle – "Ride Out"
Kidd Rock ft. Sheryl Crow – "Picture"
Gloria Gaynor – "I will Survive"
Anthony Hamilton – "I'm A Mess"
Faith Evans & Carl Thomas – "Can't Believe"
The Downtown Fiction – "I Just Want To Run"
John Mayer – "Dreaming With A Broken Heart"
Andy Grammer – "Miss me"

Part III

Keeping Him

17
Keep It Interesting

Let me hit you with some basic math. A lazy woman equals a wandering man or, worse, no man. As women we sometimes get a little complacent once we have a man in our lives. We figure the hard work of getting him is over and it shouldn't be too much more to do after we have our man. Wrong! The real work begins once we are in a relationship with that man.

Although it may seem impossible at first, you can't stop doing the things he likes when you were trying to win his love. If your hair and nails were always on point when he saw you, then the only time he should see you unkempt is when you are sleeping and even then you better not wake up looking like the bride of Frankenstein. This is why it is so important for you to keep the makeup and all those other enhancements to a minimum as mentioned in chapter 7. If you can't keep up all of that work, your man will be highly disappointed when you suddenly transform mid-relationship. I have to be honest and say that a man that truly loves you may not mind those subtle changes and may even welcome them as you being versatile. However, if you weighed 130 pounds when he met you and suddenly you are up to 180 pounds with no excuse like having a baby or being on bed rest from illness, your man may wonder what the hell happened to you. The key is to start out on a level of outward beauty that is easy for you to maintain and live up to and requires the least amount of work.

For me, even though I own tons of makeup, I wear very little. In fact, the most complicated part of my makeup routine is my individual eyelashes that I apply to make my natural lashes a little thicker. I don't get all "Miss Piggy" with the lashes to the point where I can look up and see them either. If lashes are not your thing, just try some mascara and a little bit of lip gloss with a tint. My point is that if you raise the bar too high on your man's expectations of you physically, good luck trying to jump up there and pull it back down.

One of the best ways to keep things interesting is to experience some "firsts" together. Perhaps there is some cultural event that neither of you have tried and you can both experience it for the first time and make memories that only belong to you. It's cool to go to places where you have been with other dates, but there is nothing like those places that only you and your man can call your own. The goal is to create great memories together that are just yours and his.

You may even want to hang out with other couples sometimes. You get to make some great new friends that you have something in common with seeing as though you all in "coupledom" and you get to mix things up a little. Every now and then it may get a little boring to go out by yourselves all the time, so why not go out with another couple (dating or married); especially if they are close friends of yours or his. If the relationship gets deeper, these will be the people that you will hang out with even more. Double dating puts both of you in the mindset of keeping and maintaining a relationship if you are spending time with other couples that have great relationships.

Believe it or not, men like affection too. They like to be touched, hugged and kissed sometimes just as much as women. They like it when we sneak a kiss from them in the grocery store when no one is looking or when we come up behind them and hug them while they are in front of the mirror getting ready for work or date night. Just be sure to keep the public displays of affection to a minimum. Most guys don't really like their woman totally humping their leg while you guys are in line buying windshield washer fluid for your car. Why? Believe it or not men like to keep their sex life with their woman private. Of course, that is just one reason, but the one that makes the most sense. Be tactful and respectful of him and yourself. However, you want to make that man feel loved and make sure he knows that you think he is the most desirable man in your world.

Since we are on the subject of intimacy, let me give you a hot dose of reality. Men really do want a lady in the street and a freak in the bed. Even the most quiet and reserved man will expect you to turn it up in the bedroom. If he wants you to put on a maid costume, honey you better grab a duster and strut around that house like you are getting paid to clean. Once a man is comfortable with you, or drunk, he will eventually tell you all about his hot buttons and fetishes. Now, if you are not comfortable doing something, don't attempt to do it. Not only will it be unnatural for him, but neither of you will enjoy the experience. Fulfill his requests within reason. If you don't know how to do pole tricks and he buys you a stripper pole, don't you dare touch that pole until you learn or be prepared to pull a muscle or two or even break something.

Men will not admit it, but their egos are more fragile than a woman's. If you want to keep your man happy, you better get to stroking that ego. Now, I don't mean that you should worship him, but make sure he knows that he is appreciated and needed. Not only should you thank him for the big and monumental things that he does, but also thank him for the little things that he does without even thinking. I know I have no problem thanking my man for taking out the garbage for me, checking my tire pressure or even coming to kill a bug for me. I really do appreciate him doing those things because I am sure as hell not going to do them. Even though we are taught that these are things that men are supposed to do, remind them that it doesn't go unnoticed.

By far, one of the best ways to keep things interesting in your relationship is to get the hell away from one another every now and then. If you are always up each other's ass, you will get tired of one another very quickly. Again, this goes back to that whole "get a life" thing. Give the guy some time to miss you. Go live your life and send him a "Hello" text or a quick call. Absence makes the heart grow fonder.

Keeping things interesting is what keeps your man interested. Men get bored very quickly and if you are always doing the same ole stuff, he may find someone who can keep him a little more entertained. By the way, your man should be doing his best to keep your interest as well. If being with him is turning into one long ass yawn and you really want to be with that man, give him a little heads up. If things don't get better or if he doesn't even try, perhaps you should be looking for a little more excitement too. Just remember to give him the same chance to make things better that you would want instead of immediately kicking him to the curb.

Chapter Seventeen Playlist

Johnny Gill – "My My My"

Tom Scott – "Keep This Love Alive"

Bruno Mars – "It Will Rain"

Robin Thicke – "The Sweetest Love"

Mary J. Blige – "Be Without You"

Michael Jackson – "It's The Falling In Love"

Sade – "Nothing Can Come Between Us"

Teena Marie – "Déjà vu (I've Been Here Before)"

R. Kelly – "When A Woman Loves"

Joss Stone – "Spoiled"

Whitney Houston – "Things You Say"

Lauryn Hill – "Tell Him"

Norah Jones – "Nearness Of You"

Marvin Gaye – "Sexual Healing"

Kelly Rowland ft. Lil' Wayne – Motivation

Donna Summer – "Love To Love You Baby"

Mtume – "Juicy Fruit"

Joan Jett & The Blackhearts – "Do You Wanna Touch

Teddy Pendergrass – "Turn Off The Lights"

INXS – "Need You Tonight"

Isley Brothers – "Between The Sheets"

Tim McGraw & Faith Hill – "Let's Make Love"

The Art of Noise – "Moments In Love"

Led Zepplin – "Whole Lotta Love"

K. Michelle – "V.S.O.P."

18
Communication

Bad communication or a lack thereof can be the ultimate breakdown of a relationship. If you two don't listen to one another and are never on the same page, your relationship is doomed. This will be a crash course in communicating in a relationship because there are just some things that will be unique to your relationship and you will learn along the way through trial and error.

First, let me explain how to even have a face-to-face conversation with your man. Be sure you are making eye contact to show that you are listening and really taking in everything that he has to say. How would you feel if you were talking to someone about something important and they were looking off into space as if you weren't even there or, worse, texting or playing with their cell phone? Also, make sure you are sitting next to him. Unless you can't avoid it, sitting across from him if you two must discuss an important issue could make the conversation seem more confrontational. Another thing you may want to do, but it must come natural to you, is to touch him slightly when you are talking. This lets him know you are literally "feeling" what he is saying and care about what he has to say. Last but not least, be mindful of your body language. There is a sales technique call "mirroring" that also works in normal conversations. Basically, all you are doing is mimicking your mate's body language. If he is sitting back in his chair super relaxed, you should be doing the same. People tend to open up a little more when they feel as though you are on the same emotional plane as they are. Mirroring may seem like a game, but all you are really doing is doing what it takes to keep the conversation flowing easier.

If you are talking to him over the phone about something important to one or both of you, you should be giving your full attention. You shouldn't be trying to vacuum, cook dinner and color your hair while you are on the phone. This can be very distracting and will make him think you are not paying attention and could care less about what he has to say. Not to mention, there is a good chance you will miss something very important in the conversation if you are distracted.

I personally believe that texting has ruined the art of conversation. I will admit that I text more than I call people, but when you and you mate have to talk about relationship issues, it should never be via text. A text can easily be interpreted wrong and then you will have an even bigger problem on your hands. If you need to talk about something serious, just let your man know that you would rather talk in person or over the phone so that you can both be heard. I honestly think texting should be kept to a minimum in relationships unless you are in a situation where you can't talk on the phone or you just need to send a quick message. If he is at home sitting on the couch doing nothing and you're doing the same at your house, there is no reason for you to be texting one another. Pick up the phone and talk to one another.

Now, let's get to the actual conversation. The first rule is to never speak out of anger if there is a problem. You will only say things that are hurtful and mean instead of what really needs to be said. Your man may forgive you for your not so kind words, but he will not forget them as the most truth is told when a person speaks out of anger. If you are heated about something, it is best to sit, relax, breathe and think about what you are really upset about. After you have cooled down, it is safe to talk and your mind will be clear.

While we are on the subject of anger, sometimes you have to pick your battles. Women sometimes have a way of dealing in pettiness. Let's just say everyday your man makes up the bed (for a couple living together) because he is the last one in it and when he makes the bed, it is not up to your standards. So, you get home and you start riding him about the bed being sloppy. Stop! Think about what you are really mad about and why you are starting this argument. Did you have a bad day and that messy bed is causing you to explode? Or are you mad because once again he is doing something the way he knows how and not exactly how you want it done? I think we may be on to something here. Before you start an argument like this, realize how silly it is. How many men will even attempt to make up the bed when there is a woman in the house to do it? Be glad that you have a man that will at least try to help you out around the house and let the bed just be messy unless you have guests coming over that might see it. Even better, show the poor guy how to make a bed, but do it in a way that does not come off as you "schooling" him.

If you are constantly fighting about little things like this that are easy fixes, when there is a major issue that argument could be fatal. If you are constantly yapping at your man and you finally have something real to discuss (notice I did not use the word "argue"), that might be the blow out that sends him over the edge. Why? Because you are ALWAYS on his ass. You have to learn to let the little things go and stop majoring in minors.

Another way to express your disappointment with something your man has done is to use positive reinforcement. If you really need to have what could be a heated discussion with him, you need to start off with a bit of sunshine and soften the blow to him. Let's use the messy bed as an example even though I still forbid you to bitch about it. You would start out by saying something like, "I really appreciate you helping me out around the house, but do you think you can tighten up your bed making skills?" That may seem a little lame, but it may even get a chuckle out of him and then you can take him by the hand and show him how to make the bed up then you two can mess it up together.

This is a good time to remind you that it's not what you say; it's how you say it. You may not even be looking to start an argument with your man, but the tone that you use when speaking with him may be confrontational in and of itself. Raising your voice is a sure fire way to start to ignite things. You want to talk *to* him, not *at* him. Starting off by saying, "You did ..." is a clue that there will not be a discussion, but more like an argument. Try saying something like, "When you do this... it makes me feel like..." I know it seems like some psychological mumbo jumbo, but it works. You are explaining why you are upset and how it makes you feel and you are not using an accusatory tone. Now, he will actually listen to what you have to say, because a man that loves you will not want to be the source of any pain or hurt for you. Oh and one more thing, please do not start a conversation saying, "We need to talk." There is something about those four words that send a man's heart racing and he is dreading the whole discussion even before it starts. Try something like, "Can I talk to you for a sec?" Even if you know this may be an hour-long discussion, you have created the illusion in his mind that this is a more light-hearted conversation that will not interrupt his television show.

Like I mentioned earlier in the book, women like to talk. Hell, some of us never shut up. However, if you need to really have a deep discussion with your man, you're going to have to let your teeth meet so that they can cage in your tongue. You will have to say your piece briefly and then let him respond. Oh, and you have to listen too. Don't just let him speak for the sake of letting him speak so that you can continue what you were saying. Listen to what he is saying. He will more than likely say something that will help you both get to the root of the problem. Again, let the man speak his mind because, as we all know, men are not very quick to open up and let us know what's really on their minds. Just let the man get a word in every now and then and you may be surprised what you hear.

One thing we must all stop doing as women is thinking men can read our minds. Men like to keep things simple and they want things brought to them in a direct manner. Communicating in a way that requires a man to read between the lines or try to figure out what you really mean isn't going to get you anywhere. If you have a good relationship with your man, you should be comfortable with saying what you really mean. Even if you are not a champion communicator, try your best to get your thoughts out. The more you do this, the easier it will get and the more accustomed he will become to how you express yourself. Basically, just say what you mean because men are sick of trying to figure us out.

What about ultimatums? Ultimatums have been known to further complicate and even end relationships. No one likes to be backed into a corner. In fact, being backed into a corner will cause most people to come out swinging. If you give your man an ultimatum and you are not a gambling woman, be prepared for him to do just the opposite of what you are demanding. Now, there are some times when you have no choice but to put your foot down and tell him he has to make a serious choice. But, even in that instance you must be ready for him to walk out on you. If your relationship comes down to an ultimatum, this means that things have probably become pretty hectic between you two and you both have some hard decisions to make. Bottom line, an ultimatum should never be used as a tool to simply get your way, but as the only way to get what you want or need from this man because the relationship cannot move forward without him making a choice.

The most valuable advice I can give you is to never leave each other upset. Who cares if you had a disagreement about him being late to yet another event that you two were supposed to attend together. When you part ways that night or even in the morning, you are still going to kiss him goodbye and tell him you love him because you can always finish that discussion later. I hate to put a dark cloud on this lively conversation, but you never know what could happen that would cause you to never see that person again. You don't want to feel horrible because the last thing you communicated to him was an eye roll over something stupid. You may not like that person at the moment, but that doesn't mean you don't love them.

As I first stated, communication can be the ultimate breakdown of a relationship. It takes time and a great deal of patience to learn how to communicate effectively with that special person, but once you learn to understand what drives them and what is important to them, it gets easier. You will quickly learn what to say, what not say and how to speak to them so that they are really listening to you. Relationships are hard work and the communication aspect is where most of the work is done.

Chapter Eighteen Playlist

James Ingram – "Just Once"

Maroon 5 – "Nothing Lasts Forever"

En Vogue – "Giving Him Something He Can Feel"

Jaguar Wright – "Same Shit Different Day"

Patti Labelle – "If Only You Knew"

Mary J. Blige – "No One Will Do"

Brandy ft. Kanye West – "Talk About Our Love"

Lauryn Hill – "Nothing Even Matters"

Alicia Keys – "Diary"

19
Let Him Open The Jar

A few years ago I was spending an evening at my place with the guy I was dating at the time. He was very familiar with my place and I was comfortable with him walking around and making himself at home. I was making dinner and I needed to open a jar. He was in the kitchen with me at the time and noticed that I was struggling. Of course, being a single woman and all, I had a gadget that helped me open the jar with little effort. He offered to open the jar and I quickly declined his offer showing him my cute little gadget and he watched me open the jar myself.

I noticed that he let out a little sigh and his demeanor changed for a minute, but I still wasn't aware of the fatal mistake that I had made at that moment. What I had done is made it very clear that I did not need his assistance or him for that matter. Needless to say, the relationship didn't last for many reasons, but I am positive that my never needing his help was one of the issues. In fact, I made it a point to do things for him, which was my way of 'upgrading' him. For this, I am going to credit Beyoncé (although I am a huge fan) with yet another concept that women have misinterpreted and taken to the extreme: the "Independent Woman."

What was meant to be a great song that simply made women feel good about being able to hold their own quickly turned into a "movement." Women everywhere felt like if they could pay their own bills without any help from a man, to hell with men altogether on anything else that they could do on their own. News Flash! You are supposed to be able to pay your bills without any help. It's all part of being an adult. Being independent of men has nothing to do with it. It is a wonderful thing to be able to take care of yourself and do most, if not everything, you want to do in life, but I am pretty sure this is no reason to feel an inflated sense of entitlement. Men have been taking care of themselves for years and we haven't heard one song about it. What I am trying to get at is kudos to all women and men who can take care of themselves, but that is not a badge that you wear to exclude someone from your life.

Now that I have told you what independence is really all about, I can help you to come down off of your pedestal and keep from scaring away some poor guy who only wanted to be a gentleman and show you how much he cares about you. The bottom line is if a man does not feel needed, he will not stick around. This does not mean totally laying down and playing dead or the damsel in distress, but trying to balance a strong sense of independence and make a man feel like you want him to stick around can be a little tricky. You don't want to push him away with actions and words that make it obvious that he is nowhere near being your knight in shining armor. You also don't want to come off as totally needy as this is worse than pumping your fist in the air and declaring your independence right in front of him.

One of the most surprising results from my surveys and roundtable discussions was that most men and women aren't looking for someone who brings home a lot of bacon. What this means is that men are not looking for "Miss. I-Can-Pay-For-Everything." They are looking for a mate who is intelligent, potential and strives to do great things. How simple is that? All this time we have been busting our butts to get as many degrees as possible so that we can add as many zeros as possible to our paychecks and buy big houses, luxury cars and all the designer clothes that our closets can hold and men just want a woman who can hold a conversation, think her way out of a paper bag and pursue her own dreams. In fact, when I asked men what turned them on about a woman, not one of them said a high income, a big house, and the ability to open a jar on her own.

What can definitely turn a man off is a woman who is too dependent on him. Constantly having your hand out for things that you should be able to do on your own will send any man running. Many of us have had times when it was hard making ends meet and needed a little help. Men understand this, but if you can *never* pay your rent without his help or you can and you just keep hitting him up just because you can, you may be headed for a breakup. By constantly needing help to take care of yourself, you are sending a message that you may not be relationship material because you may not be able to pick up where he left off if he is unable to provide for the household. Men do not mind a woman who occasionally asks for help with little things. It's the constant pressure to take care of a woman who may never be able to do for herself that gives them pause. What's interesting is many men will figure out what your needs are if you have let them into your world enough. They will know that you need some extra money to get your car fixed, a new refrigerator or even a day to relax at a spa after a rough week. Just be careful about leaning on him too much for your own good and his. There is nothing like being able to take care of yourself as well as having a man around to give you a little boost if you truly need it.

Most "real men" are not intimidated by a woman who is more educated than they are or who makes more money. What turns them off is a woman who constantly makes them aware that she is more intelligent and makes more money. I don't care if that man is sitting at home taking care of the babies while you bring home seven or eight figures, it is wrong to make him feel like he is less of a man because he is not "making it rain" in the household. Most women would have a fit if they were a stay-at-home wife and they were made to feel like second-class citizens in their own homes. So don't treat your man as if he is nothing when you *think* you have the upper hand.

Now before you slam this book shut and curse my name, I am not telling you to bow down and let the man just completely take over. I am simply telling you to let a man be a man. Let him do all of those things that you may have watched your own father or other men do for the women in their lives. Let him open the door for you. Let him pump the gas. Let him pay for dinner. Let him fix all the crap that you broke around the house. Even if he still wants to rub your feet after you just got a pedicure, let him do it. Just let the man open the damn jar!

Chapter Nineteen Playlist

Sade – "Love Is Stronger Than Pride"

Timothy Bloom ft. V – 'Til the End of Time"

Toni Braxton – "You Mean The World To Me"

Tim McGraw – "Real Good Man"

Usher – "Trading Places"

R. Kelly – "Imagine That"

Salt-n-Pepa – "What A Man"

End
The Fuss is over!

There are exceptions to a lot of tips in this book. Again, I am not a certified relationship expert. Is there even such a thing? What I do know is that we learn from our experiences and dating is definitely full of trial and error. Your dating life should be full of new and exciting experiences. Sure, some of those experiences are going to be a little hurtful or even heartbreaking, but you must pick yourself up, dust yourself off and move on with your increased knowledge. Dating does not always lead to marriage. Every man you date is not meant to be your husband or anybody's husband for that matter. My final message is to have fun out there in the dating world, ease up on yourself and when the right man comes along, you will know it and you will know how to keep him in your life; especially if he wants to stay there.

Acknowledgements

Let me first give thanks to God and the spirituality that I have found. Without it, I would not have had the clearness of mind to write this book.

To Ricardo Medina (My Divo!) and the Luxury Management team, you all are absolutely fabulous.

Special thanks to Professor Paul Gaszak for lending me your extraordinary editing talents. You helped it all make sense and flow without me having to change my voice.

Although I came up with the majority of the playlist songs, I most definitely had some input from friends. Thanks to Marcus Chavers, Jason Lloyd, John Branch, Carrie Lara, Marianne Kerrigan, Julie Reincke, Cassi Petrusevski, Stacy McGury, Britney Sanders-Fields, Sharae Smith, Arthur Oates, Tina Perkins, Nicole Koskovich, Shatonda Perkins-Stallworth, Therese Welch, Marco Mallard, Krystal Nelson, Sheherazade Robinson, Yolanda Minott and I hope I didn't miss anyone but you know I still love you.

www.ingramcontent.com/pod-product-compliance
Lightning Source LLC
Chambersburg PA
CBHW061646040426
42446CB00010B/1609